CW00350574

Best Pub Walks in the White Peak

2nd edition © Les Lumsdon and Martin Smith, 2012

1st edition © Les Lumsdon and Martin Smith, 2005

All Rights Reserved. No part of this publication may be reproduced, stored in a retrieval system, or transmitted in any form or by any means – electronic, mechanical, photocopying, recording, or otherwise – without prior written permission from the publisher or a licence permitting restricted copying issued by the Copyright Licensing Agency, 90 Tottenham Court Road, London W1P 0LA. This book may not be lent, resold, hired out or otherwise disposed of by trade in any form of binding or cover other than that in which it is published, without the prior consent of the publisher.

Moral Rights: The Authors have asserted their moral rights to be identified as the Authors of this Work.

Published by Sigma Leisure – an imprint of
Sigma Press, Stobart House, Pontyclerc, Penybanc Road, Ammanford, Carmarthenshire SA18 3HP.

British Library Cataloguing in Publication Data
A CIP record for this book is available from the British Library.

ISBN: 978-1-85058-933-4

Typesetting and Design by: Sigma Press, Ammanford, Carms

Cover photograph: The Church Inn, Chelmorton © Les Lumsdon

Photographs: © Martin Smith

Maps: Bute Cartographics. Reproduced by permission of Ordnance Survey on behalf of HMSO ©Crown Copyright 2005. Ordnance Survey licence number 100032058

Printed by: TJ International Ltd, Padstow, Cornwall

Disclaimer: the information in this book is given in good faith and is believed to be correct at the time of publication. No responsibility is accepted by either the author or publisher for errors or omissions, or for any loss or injury howsoever caused. Only you can judge your own fitness, competence and experience. Do not rely solely on sketch maps for navigation: we strongly recommend the use of appropriate Ordnance Survey (or equivalent) maps.

Best Pub Walks in the White Peak

Les Lumsdon & Martin Smith

Acknowledgements

The authors wish to gratefully acknowledge the assistance of a number of people in the preparation of this edition of the White Peak pub walks book. In particular, we would like to thank those friends and colleagues who either researched the walks themselves or accompanied one or other of the authors on their travels. Not that reconnoitring the walks or, more particularly the pubs, proved to be a great chore! These people are, in alphabetical order: Chris Morris, Eva Haake-Heil, Howard and Anne Smith, John and Margaret Manning, Mike and Jane Nelms, Robin Lumb, Tony and Maureen Corker, Tom and Helen.

An especial mention must be made of Margaret and Maureen, who had the unenviable task of reading through the text and pointing out inconsistencies and discrepancies.

Preface

The Peak District is well walked and given the outstanding beauty of the landscape, its history and culture, this is hardly surprising. The network of paths is, for the most part, in good order. This is a great bonus for walkers who may be used to finding their local paths in less desirable conditions. In contrast, the Peak District seems something of a paradise, but it will only remain so if we collectively seek to protect it by supporting the conservation work of local landowners, voluntary groups, the National Park and the local councils. They contend with over twenty million visitors every year and this cannot be an easy task. Being a considerate visitor is very important.

Given the increasing number of pubs that are going out of business, we were agreeably surprised to find that, when we revised this book in 2012, only one of the pubs mentioned in previous editions had succumbed, and even that was not one of our featured pubs. Do your bit to keep the rural pub going, because one of the bonuses of enjoying a walk is to adjourn to a local hostelry for a good pint of ale (or some other beverage) or simply as a respite part way along the route. Inns have for centuries welcomed customers on foot, be they trades people, farmers going to and from market, or, nowadays, lovers of the countryside seeking their leisure pursuits at weekends. Long may the tradition of hospitality and good ale remain. For the latter we must thank the excellent work of CAMRA, the Campaign for Real Ale, in championing the cause of real ale and supporting rural public houses. Take a look at their website, **www.camra.org.uk** for more information.

Of course, for the rambler who loves real ale there's one snag – beer and driving do not mix. All the walks in this book feature at least one pub, so those who like a drop or two should either let someone else do the driving, or, better still, use the local bus. In so doing you will be doing your bit to keep the rural bus network going and helping to reduce car congestion on the roads and in the villages.

The walks in this volume feature the central part of the Peak District, known as the White Peak. There's a companion volume for the Dark Peak. Together, these two books offer a wide range of walks across the Peak District.
Happy rambling!

Les Lumsdon and Martin Smith

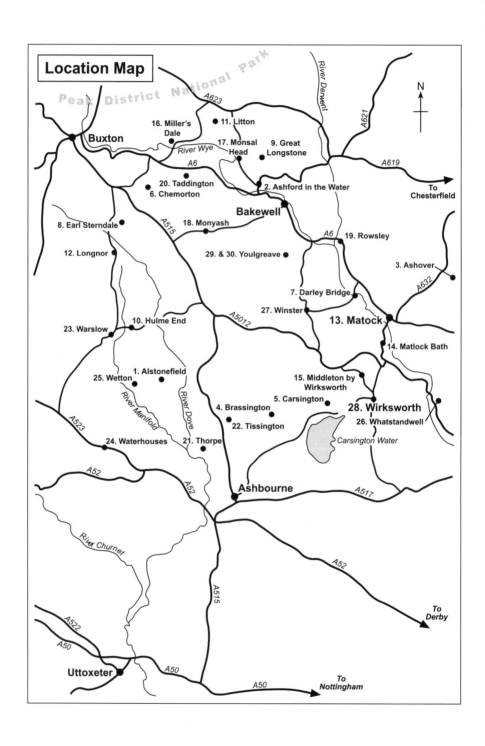

Contents

The Peak District and its Pubs   9
The Peak District   9
Ancient Sites   10
Lost Villages   10
Green and Gold   11
Subterranean Blues   11
Lead Mining   12
Routes   13
Peakland Customs   13
The Walks   14
The Pubs   15
Be Prepared   16
                                            17

The Walks

Walk 1. Alstonefield   Distance: 6¼ miles (10 km)   19

Walk 2. Ashford in the Water Distance: 5½ miles (9¼ km)   26

Walk 3. Ashover   Distance: 4 miles (6½ km)   32

Walk 4. Brassington   Distance: 4.7 miles (7.6 km)   40

Walk 5. Carsington   Distance: 8½ miles (13.7 km)   47

Walk 6. Chelmorton   Distance: 5.6 miles (9 km)   54

Walk 7. Darley Bridge   Distance: 5.1 miles (8¼ km)   60

Walk 8. Earl Sterndale   Distance: 5.4 miles (8.6 km)   68

Walk 9. Great Longstone   Distance: 8 miles (12.9 km)   73

Walk 10. Hulme End   Distance: 4½ miles (7¼ km)   82

Walk 11. Litton   Distance: 5.1 miles (8.1km)   87

Walk 12. Longnor to Hartington Distance: 5.6 miles (9 km)   95

Walk 13. Matlock   Distance: 4¼ miles (7 km)   102

Walk 14. Matlock Bath   Distance: 5.6 miles (9 km)   109

Walk 15. Middleton by Wirksworth   Distance: 5.2 miles (8.4 km)   118

Walk 16. Miller's Dale   Distance: 5.3 miles (8½ km)   127

Walk 17. Monsal Head   Distance: 5.3 miles (8½ km)   132

Walk 18. Monyash   Distance: 4.1 miles (6.6 km)   138

Walk 19. Rowsley and Stanton in Peak   Distance: 6.7 miles (10.8 km)   144

Walk 20. Taddington   Distance: 5.2 miles (8.4 km)   152

Walk 21. Thorpe   Distance: 4¾ miles (7.7 km)   156

Walk 22. Tissington   Distance: 5¼ miles (8.5 km)   161

Walk 23. Warslow   Distance: 3.8 miles (6.2 km)   166

Walk 24. Waterhouses   Distance: 6.3 miles (10.2 km)   171

Walk 25. Wetton   Distance: 4 miles (6.5 km)   179

Walk 26. Whatstandwell   Distance: 6.1 miles (9.8 km)   183

Walk 27. Winster   Distance: 3.9 miles (6¼ km)   190

Walk 28. Wirksworth   Distance: 5 miles (8 km)   197

Walk 29. Youlgreave (Bradford Dale)   Distance: 3.9 miles (6.3 km)   205

Walk 30. Youlgreave to Bakewell   Distance: 4¼ miles (6¾ km)   211
   via Over Haddon

The Peak District and its Pubs

The exact boundaries of the Peak District are the subject of some debate. Certainly the towns of Buxton and Matlock would regard themselves as part of it, having for at least two centuries used their Peak District associations to attract visitors to good effect. The boundaries of the Peak District National Park however, are more tightly defined. The National Park leaves out the Matlocks and Buxton's of this world, plus much fine countryside that many would argue is of National Park standard, e.g. around Wirksworth, Ashbourne and Matlock.

Perhaps it is better to simply define the Peak District as that area of countryside, moorland and dale, lying between the conurbations of Manchester, Sheffield, the Potteries and Derby. Certainly this is how the visitor tends to regard it.

The area covered by this book is mainly the limestone part of the Peak District known as the White Peak, though the surrounding gritstone moors and edges are included. We treat the Peak District's boundaries in an even more liberal fashion, by including walks in Crich and Ashover, which few of the most expansionist of Peak District devotees would regard as being within the area. A companion book covers the Dark Peak, the area north of the Hope Valley.

We have to recognise that for many people the Peak District is home; the place where they live and work; a hard existence farming the hills in some cases. Most of all it is an ancient land, rich in human culture and in the patterns of its landscape. It is a land to enjoy but respect, to husband and conserve for future generations.

What better way to discover such a landscape than on foot?

The Peak District

The Peak District is probably more conscious of its past than most other regions in England. Its past has not been buried in a welter of rebuilding. The isolation and ruggedness of the landscape and the harshness of the climate have served to ensure that ample evidence of the earliest inhabitants and their various successors remains, in a way that is remarkable.

One may well ask why this area, so devoid of mountains and peaked hills, is called The Peak? The truth seems to be that the earliest name was Peac-lond, meaning the country where the Pecsaetan people dwelt. The origins of this tribe are obscure, opinion being divided on whether they were of pre- or post-Roman origin. Equally, the boundaries of their territory are uncertain. Southwards their influence probably ceased somewhere between Crich and

Belper. Eastwards it possibly stretched over to the valleys of the Don and Rother, whilst to the west it maybe finished where the tumbling slopes of Shining Tor meet the Cheshire plain.

Ancient Sites

Although there's now strong evidence of early settlement on the high gritstone moors, it seems likely that our original Peac-londers must have concentrated on the southern (limestone) part of their territory. There are many remains of early man in the White Peak: fortresses, burial sites, dwellings and great ceremonial sites such as Arbor Low. Our earliest known trackways date from these pre-Roman times, and linked these centres of population and culture. Many of these routes still survive and some are incorporated into the walks in this book.

The Roman occupation seems also to have concentrated on the limestone part of the Peak. Here they mined and smelted lead, built their homes and bathhouses, their forts and highways. The immediate post-Roman period in the Peak is almost a complete mystery, but it is a fallacy to suppose that the Saxons charged in as the last legionaries marched out. There could well have been two hundred years or so before the final imposition of Saxon rule.

The Romano-British culture therefore survived well into the Saxon period. There's evidence for this in place and river names like Eccles and Derwent. Later conquerors like the Danes and the Normans laid a veneer on the ancient bones of the Peak, adding their castles and settlements but retaining sprawling Christian parishes such as Hope.

Lost Villages

Huge tracts of the Peak became royal hunting forest in Norman times, and were subject to harsh forest law. The village of Peak Forest is a reminder of this, as is Peveril Castle and the name of the pub in Hope, the Woodruffe Arms, a corruption of Wood reeve, one of the principal enforcers of forest law. In the Middle Ages, sometimes known as The Age of Faith, mining and agricultural development flourished, but the onset of the Black Death and other bouts of plague altered the farming pattern substantially and some villages vanished altogether.

With the onset of the agrarian and industrial revolutions in the 18th century, the scene changed dramatically again. It seems that enclosure started early on the limestone uplands and some villages retain the fossilised remains of their mediaeval strip fields defined by limestone walls. The walk from Chelmorton is a must for those who are interested in this aspect. Elsewhere, vast tracts of hitherto open land were enclosed, water-powered mills were constructed; many roads were widened and straightened. Indeed there were more roads built in the Peak District in the 18th and 19th centuries than during the motor age in which we now live and most of the present main road network dates from this period. This left the older routes far less busy and some reverted to mere tracks and paths. Canals made no impact on the heart of Peakland, though not for want of trying. Their railway successors however, left indelible marks, with their cuttings and embankments, their viaducts and tunnels. Many of these lines are now gone, greatly lamented by those who grew up with railway travel, but in their place have come the railway trails, very popular walking and cycling routes.

Green and Gold

The Peak District is the start of the Pennines, known as the "backbone of England". At their southern end, the area covered by this book, the Pennines decline gently into the Midland plain. The hills are threaded with walls and often crowned with trees. The fields offer shades of green and gold. Many deep and narrow dales dissect the limestone plateau of the White Peak. These valleys are well hidden from the surrounding land and each one has a very different character.

The southernmost part of the Peak District is chiefly in Derbyshire, but it does encompass parts of the Staffordshire Moorlands. The hills are not high and to confuse matters are often called "Lows". This is a corruption of the Norse "hlaw", meaning hill, and not an example of Derbyshire understatement! The hills lack the stark grandeur of the Lake District or Snowdonia, but the broad sweeping moorlands and the limestone plateau have an appeal all of their own.

The southern Peak has its drama in the form of the eastern edges, a barrier of gritstone cliffs stretching all along the Derwent valley, unique in Britain for their length. The views eastwards along the Hope Valley to Millstone Edge and Surprise are a magnificent sight, especially when the cliffs catch the rays of the setting sun.

These gritstone edges and outcrops have long been the playground of the rock climber. More recently the huge scattered gritstone boulders beneath the edges and the precipitous limestone cliffs of Stoney Middleton and Matlock Bath have also become increasingly popular with climbers.

The limestone landscape has other appeals too. The view of the reef hills of the Upper Dove from Crowdecote is a true delight, whilst the rock pinnacles of Dove Dale and the towering cliffs of High Tor will cause an admiring intake of breath. It may be a gentler landscape, but it has real beauty for the walker.

Subterranean Blues

Not all of the Peak District's beauties lie on the surface. The limestone is riddled with subterranean passages and caves, some natural, others extended by man in search of minerals like lead or the famous Blue John stone. Many of these caverns can be visited in perfect safety in the show caves of Matlock Bath and Castleton. The work of the miner and quarryman is explained to good effect at the Peak District Mining Museum in Matlock Bath and the National Stone Centre in Wirksworth.

It is probably in the valleys that the southern Peak District is at its best. Some wind for miles, tree clad, narrow and secretive. Most are dry dales, though originally water carved. Some retain their rivers, which have charmed poets and writers through the centuries. The very sound of the waterfalls is music. Some of the rivers are seasonal, vanishing altogether in summer and becoming foaming torrents in winter. Disappearing rivers are a feature of limestone territory and the elusive Manifold and Lathkill are classic examples. Several of the walks in this book venture into these dales, rich in wildlife and host to a number of rare plant species.

Lead Mining

The White Peak is an area of industrial as well as natural interest, exemplified in the remains of lead mining. Many of the public rights of way mentioned in the text owe their existence to the mining industry, as routes to work or for the transporting of ore to the smelters and from the smelters to markets in the east and south. Be careful not to stray from the paths in mining areas. Most of the old shafts have been capped by Derbyshire County Council, but some have not and they are dangerous.

The story of lead mining and lead itself is fascinating. The tale begins some 330 million years ago, when much of the southern part of the Peak was a shallow tropical sea, with coral reefs and myriads of shellfish. Their shells formed the limestone. There were volcanoes in the area and periodically outbursts of lava covered the ocean floors and killed the corals and shellfish. Remains of the lava flows can still be discerned in places. The Bonsall walk passes a good example at Masson.

The limestone was folded and cracked over millions of years and the resultant gaps filled with various minerals associated with lead; fluorspar, calcite and barytes, the very stuff of the geography and geology class room practical. The minerals were formed about 180 million years ago, carried by hot volcanic fluids, which as they cooled deposited the various minerals in the cracks and caverns. Well over 100 different minerals, some of considerable rarity, have been recorded in the Peak District mines. The mineral filled vertical faults and cracks in the limestone may run for miles and are known as "rakes", or in a smaller version, "scrins". Where the limestone was sandwiched between lava flows the mineral takes the form of "flats". These are more like a coal seam, but usually much thinner and rarely very extensive. Where the mineral filled caverns, the result was known as a "pipe". Masson cavern at Matlock Bath is the best-known example and can be readily visited.

It seems likely that lead mining was going on in the area before the Roman occupation, but the demands of Imperial Rome carried the industry to new heights (or depths). Lead was mined and smelted extensively in the Matlock and Bradwell areas and lead ingots, known as "pigs" were transported eastwards to the Rivers Idle and Trent for shipment.

A whole body of law was laid down about this time to govern the working of the industry. It says much for the importance of the Derbyshire ore field that a version of Roman mining law survived as an oral tradition through the Dark Ages into Saxon and Norman England, finally receiving written status in the "Quo Warranto" of 1287. This law was finally enshrined in Acts of Parliament in the early 1850s and still forms the basis for mineral mining law in the Peak District today.

Routes

Finally let us look at those historical features without which this book would be impossible. We take the footpath and road network very much for granted and likewise the public houses along these routes. We think little of the origins of such features, but it is worth remembering that before the 20th century, the only people to travel any distance for leisure were the rich and walking any distance for pleasure was not fashionable. The local road and footpath network was developed essentially for economic purposes, a route from village to mine, from farm to market, from village to town, from hamlet to parish church. Successive transport improvements and changes in working patterns have enhanced the status of some routes beyond all recognition, from country lane to major highway. Conversely other routes have become economically redundant, surviving now only for leisure purposes. These highways of the past are now our walking routes. Fortunately, since we first penned the earlier version of this book in the 1990s, the footpaths, bridleways and "green lanes" have remained largely intact, although increasing usage by off-road vehicles has caused considerable damage in some cases.

Peakland Customs

The Peak District is well known for its customs. By far the best known and most picturesque is the dressing of the wells in various villages. Each participating village painstakingly prepares a picture made of natural materials such as flowers, twigs, moss, leaves and bark, on a clay base. This is displayed at or near a village well or spring as a thanksgiving for pure water. Several villages have week long ceremonies and events surrounding the well dressings and these are very popular with visitors. Tissington, the starting point for a walk to Parwich and also included in the Thorpe walk, used to be the first of the season. It is probably still the best known, though many other villages, even some outside the Peak District, have now developed the tradition and they are all worth visiting. There are other well-established events such as Flagg races (see the Chelmorton walk) and some strange customs like the legendary Bonsall hen races (see Matlock walk).

The Walks

There are thirty walks, with lengths varying from 3½ to 8½ miles (6 to 14km). All the walks include at least one public house. Some walks are a veritable drinker's paradise, with a choice of pubs. In these cases, and indeed any instance where you are intending to quaff ale, do the travelling to and from the walk by bus or train, or get someone else to do the driving. Each walk includes details of how to reach the starting point by public transport. Most of the walks are circular (roughly) but two are linear and for these you need to use the bus. The White Peak is mostly well-blessed with bus services (and a local railway line, the Matlock branch), all of which have seen increased frequency and some attractive ticket initiatives over the last few years.

The county councils are keen to encourage use of these services and most of them are daily. You may be used to the urban bus or not use them at all. Try not to judge the rural bus in the same light. It is very different. The routes are scenic and the bus operators pride themselves on reliability. Some of the companies have picked up awards for their customer care and quality, such as Trent Barton. The main arterial route is the Trans Peak (TP) between Derby and Manchester. The walks from Chelmorton, Taddington, Ashford, Rowsley, Darley Bridge, Matlock, Matlock Bath and Whatstandwell are accessible from this route. There are some unsung heroes working other routes too. The ride between Ashbourne and Buxton on service 442 has to be one of the most understated for panoramic views. The walks from Earl Sterndale, Longnor, Tissington, Thorpe and Warslow are served by this route. To sum up, public transport in the Peak District still remains good, though it is under threat from cut backs in local authority budgets, but with the daunting prospect of worsening effects of climatic change, the reduction of car travel makes sense.

Public transport information for the whole of the Peak District can be obtained from Traveline (0871 200 22 33) or by checking the Derbyshire County Council public transport website: **www.derbyshire.gov.uk/buses**. The Peak District Bus Timetable is the bible of all bus timetables. It is exceptional value for the walker and is updated regularly or by checking the website. It is possible to buy the book at local Tourist Information Centres. There are also booklets and route specific leaflets available, including one detailing the Derbyshire train services. For information about public transport to any of the places mentioned in this book go to **www.travelineeastmidlands.org.uk**.

The Pubs

The pub is a much-loved institution and in many rural areas we are losing them at a fast rate. Some seek to convert them into dwellings for financial gain regardless of the desires of local communities, but where there are enough residents and visitors, well-run local pubs seem to flourish. It is clearly the case that since we first walked these routes, most pubs have moved towards the provision of food or have established dining rooms where customers can enjoy a meal in more formal surroundings. Thankfully, this has not been, in most cases, to the complete loss of a pub atmosphere in pursuit of a restaurant format. Most pubs have simply got better at offering good food in addition to a wide range of beverages, including teas, coffees as well as real ales. Many have remained firstly as the village local, but also hold out a welcome to the visitor. In some cases, the publicans we have contacted also like a local walk. In more than one place the landlord is known to lead occasional guided walks. Wherever possible we highlight whether the pub prefers you to kick your boots off (perhaps not literally) or to use boot covers. Please respect the customs of the pub, especially with regard to wearing boots, admittance of children and dogs.

We give opening times of the featured pubs, where we have been able to establish this. Some pubs close on certain weekdays or at least don't open at lunchtimes. We have given telephone numbers of each featured pub and, where possible their website address. We strongly advise that you check beforehand, especially if you want a lunchtime meal and drink.

The Peak District is also home to a number of enterprising micro-breweries. In the White Peak the main offerings have, for some time, come from the Whim brewery, located near to Hartington, and Thornbridge brewery in Bakewell, both of which are exceptional brews. However, more recent arrivals include beers from the Buxton Brewery and Peak Ales from the Chatsworth Estate. These now make for a great range of locally crafted brews The owner of the Leek brewery (bottled beers only) also enjoys a good walk and refers to the likes of us as "drinkers with a walking problem". All well and good, but many of the small breweries are still crowded out of pubs because of distribution deals or supply restrictions with many of the pub companies, so whenever you find a guest ale from one of the small breweries – try a pint! We give details of the beers served at the featured pubs, but these cannot be taken for granted, especially at free houses and the many pubs where guest beers are on offer. These change quite rapidly. If you want to find out what's on offer, you are advised to check with the pub beforehand.

The table on the following two pageslists all the featured pubs and gives their telephone numbers and websites, where available.

Be Prepared

When setting out for a day in the countryside, it is worth remembering the old motto, "Be Prepared". A rucksack with a waterproof and some warm clothing prepares you for a change in the weather. If you are out for any length of time take a snack with you and a small first aid kit. Both are light to carry, but could prove important. Stout footwear is vital. People have been known to break ankles even on gentle walks and some of these walks are far from sedate. Boots are preferable, for some walks can be muddy, though many walkers use good trainers during the summer months. You shouldn't need reminding to take a decent map. Each individual walk states which map is required. Most of the walks in the book can be done using the OS 1:25000 Explorer 0L24 White Peak map. The latest version shows the new Access areas. We have also given rough times for completion of the walks. Times are based on the good old Naismith formula, 3 miles per hour and half an hour per 1000 feet of ascent. For the metricated of our readers, that's about 5kph and half an hour per 300m of ascent.

Pub Contact Details

Walk	The Pub	Location	Website	Telephone
Walk 1	The George	Alstonefield	www.thegeorge@alstonefield.com	01335 310205
Walk 2	Bull's Head	Ashford in the Water		01629 812931
	Cock and Pullet	Sheldon		01629 814292
Walk 3	Old Poets' Corner	Ashover	www.oldpoets.co.uk	01246 590888
	Black Swan	Ashover	www.blackswanashover.co.uk	01246 591926
	The Crispin	Ashover		01246 590911
Walk 4	Miners Arms	Brassington		01629 540222
	Ye Olde Gate	Brassington	www.yeoldegateinnbrassington.co.uk	01629 540448
Walk 5	Miners Arms	Carsington	www.minersarmscarsington.co.uk	01629 540207
Walk 6	Church Inn	Chelmorton	www.thechurchinn.co.uk	01298 85319
	Duke of York	Pomeroy	www.thedukeofyorkpub.com	01298 83345
Walk 7	Square and Compass	Darley Bridge	www.thesquareandcompass.co.uk	01629 733255
Walk 8	Quiet Woman	Earl Sterndale		01298 83211
Walk 9	Crispin Inn	Great Longstone	www.thecrispingreatlongstone.co.uk	01629 640237
	White Lion	Great Longstone	www.whiteliongreatlongstone.co.uk	01629 640252
	Packhorse	Little Longstone	www.packhorselongstone.co.uk	01629 640471
Walk 10	Manifold Inn	Hulme End	www.themanifoldinn.co.uk	01298 84537
	Staffordshire Knot	Sheen	www.thestaffordshireknot.co.uk	01298 84329
Walk 11	Red Lion	Litton	www.theredlionlitton.co.uk	01298 871458
Walk 12	Packhorse	Crowdecote	www.thepackhorseinn.co.uk	01298 83618
	Charles Cotton	Hartington	www.charlescotton.co.uk	01298 84229
Walk 13	Kings Head	Bonsall	www.bonsallvillage.org	01629 822703
	Barley Mow	Bonsall	www.barleymowbonsall.co.uk	01629 825685

Walk	The Pub	Location	Website	Telephone
Walk 14	Princess Victoria	Matlock Bath	www.princessvic.co.uk	01629 593458
Walk 15	Rising Sun	Middleton by Wirksworth	www.risingsuninn.co.uk	01629 822420
Walk 16	Angler's Rest	Miller's Dale	www.theanglersrest.co.uk	01298 871323
Walk 17	Monsal Head Hotel	Monsal Head	www.monsalhead.com	01629 640250
Walk 18	The Bull's Head	Monyash	www.thebullsheadmonyash.co.uk	01629 812372
Walk 19	Flying Childers	Stanton-in-the-Peak	www.flyingchilders.com	01629 636333
Walk 20	Queens Arms	Taddington	www.queensarmstaddington.com	01298 85245
Walk 21	Coach and Horses	Fenny Bentley		01335 350246
Walk 22	The Sycamore	Parwich		01335 390212
Walk 23	The Greyhound	Warslow	www.greyhoundinnwarslow.co.uk	01298 687017
	The Black Lion	Butterton	www.blacklioninn.co.uk	01538 304232
Walk 24	Red Lion	Waterfall	www.peaklion.co.uk	01538 308279
	Ye Olde Crown	Waterhouses	www.homepage.ntlworld.com	01538 308204
Walk 25	Ye Olde Royal Oak	Wetton	www.royaloakwetton.co.uk	01335 310287
Walk 26	Cliff Inn	Crich	www.thecliffinn.co.uk	01773 852444
	Black Swan	Crich		01773 852026
Walk 27	The Miners Standard	Winster Bank Top	www.theminersstandard.com	01629 650279
Walk 28	Black's Head	Wirksworth	www.blackshead.co.uk	01629 823257
	Hope and Anchor	Wirksworth	www.hopenanchor.co.uk	01629 823340
Walk 29	George Hotel	Youlgreave		01629 636292
Walk 30	Lathkil Hotel	Over Haddon	www.lathkil.co.uk	01629 812501

Walk 1. Alstonefield

The route	Alstonefield, Hopedale, Stanshope, Hall Dale, Ilam Rock, Dove Holes, Milldale, Lode Mill, Coldeaton Bridge, Gipsy Bank, Alstonefield
Distance	6¼ miles (10 km). 1735 feet of ascent (529 metres). Allow 3½ to 4 hours, exclusive of stops. Opportunity for short cut from Milldale, saving 1¼ miles (2 km) and 400 feet (120 metres) of climbing
Grade	Hard, with a couple of significant climbs
Start	Alstonefield Village Car Park and Toilets. Map reference: 137551
Map	OS Explorer OL 24 The Peak District, White Peak
How to get there by bus	The demand responsive service, Moorlands Connect serves Alstonefield on Mondays to Saturdays, telephone 0300 1118003 for details. Service High Peak 42A (Ashbourne-Buxton) serves Alstonefield on Sundays and Bank Holidays. There's a daily service (High Peak 42 and 442) along the A515 between Buxton and Ashbourne, calling at Newton House from which point it is a 15 minute walk down to Lode Mill (0.8 miles/1¼ km) and a 25 minute walk back up (same distance but 338 feet/103 metres ascent)
How to get there by car	Alstonefield is signed from Hulme End on the B5054 road from Hartington or from the main A515 road between Ashbourne and Buxton. There's a small car park and toilet block in the village, so please park there

The Pub

The George (tel: 01335 310205), alongside Alstonefield village green, is justifiably popular with walkers visiting this part of the Staffordshire Moorlands in the very south of the Peak District. On many a winter's day, rows of boots (everyone is asked to remove walking boots) and cagoules can be seen lined up in the outer porch, with ramblers inside warming their spirits by the fire either mid way or after a walk. It is said the pub dates back to the coaching era, but there was also much market activity around the village. There was evidently a wool market to the rear of the pub. The pub has two main rooms and the relatively low ceilings and beams add to the character of the place, as do the pictures of the southern Peak. To the rear of the pub, there's also a campsite, which is available for families.

The George sells a range of real ales. Families are welcome. There are also seats outside of the pub overlooking the village green.

Opening Times: Monday to Thursday: 11.30am-3pm & 6pm-11pm, Friday and Saturday: 11.30am-11pm, Sunday: 12pm-9.30pm

The Walk

The village of Alstonefield is one of the loveliest of the Staffordshire Moorlands area. The church is of great antiquity – the direction sign says it's 12th century, but it has been much restored over the years. Two scholars and friends of note, Charles Cotton and Izaak Walton worshipped here and there's a pew and pulpit belonging to Cotton, which can still be viewed. Near to the church are Alstonefield Hall, (dating from the late 16th century) and a splendid Georgian rectory. All of these are within a short stroll of the village green.

Don't bank on Harry

From the car park by the toilet block go right. Bear left at the road junction and so reach the village green. Go right here and pass the George Inn. No deviating at this stage. Head straight past the George to the signed footpath situated to the right of Bumblies Barn. A stile takes you into open fields. With a wall to your left, go through a series of stiles until you come to a crossing of paths. Go straight on, across the field to another stile, marked with a signpost. In this next field, you cross another path and bear right, heading down the field into Hopedale. In the bottom right hand corner of the field there's a large tree and here you reach the top of Harry's Bank and the start of the descent to Dale Bottom. A well-trodden bridleway leads down Harry's Bank, which is serious stuff in winter for it becomes something of a quagmire on slippery limestone. There's a signed alternative zigzag path down the hillside, but this is little better than the direct route. Either way, tread with care. The direct route leads to a stile out onto the lane. Opposite, a little to the left, is a continuation of your route. Cross the lane and begin the climb up a far less muddy track to Stanshope. The track levels and passes by Grove and Church Farms to reach the road which threads through the hamlet, with Stanshope Hall to your right.

Descent of Hall Dale

Turn left at the road in front of Stanshope Hall and then almost immediately left again down a walled track signposted to Milldale and Dovedale via Hall

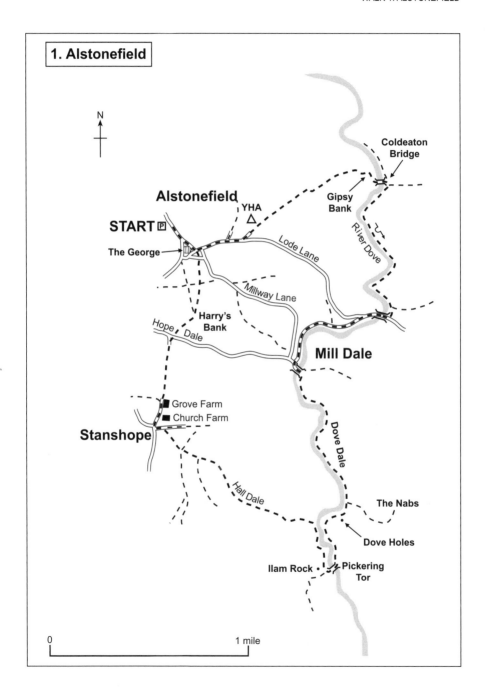

1. Alstonefield

Dale. About 100 yards/metres down this lane go right, through a gate/stile signed to Hall Dale.

Beware! After heavy rain the puddle on the field side of this gate is deeper than you might think – believe me.

The path across the field is obvious and it passes through a series of stiles/gates into the narrowing confines of Hall Dale, the jaws of which can be seen ahead.

Hall Dale is a dry dale, which means that there's no permanent stream in it. It does not mean that there's no mud or puddles after heavy rain and when this walk was recce'd if there had been a spell of that sort of weather so the descent was not without interest! The scenery is very impressive as you descend further and further into the dale. At some points you could almost reach out and touch the rock walls on either side, and then, just as suddenly, the dale widens out again.

A final steep descent on bare limestone brings you to the banks of the River Dove and the boundary between Staffordshire and Derbyshire.

Most of the time, the Dove is a placid, archetypal trout stream, described as such in Walton's "Compleat Angler". This was not the case when the walk was recce'd. The roaring, foaming brown torrent looked and sounded very impressive and not a little frightening.

As you face the river there's a signpost that directs you to the right to Ilam Rock Bridge (¼ mile).

To the left is another path, unsigned, except for a small wooden notice. On closer examination the notice suggests that the path ahead is difficult and impassable after heavy rain. One look at the river in front of you will tell you whether to venture on this alternative route. We didn't.

Along Dove Dale to Milldale

Even if you have a mind to try the west bank alternative, it is worth following the signed path to Ilam Rock, which is very impressive as are the rock spires on the east bank. As for climbing Ilam Rock, forget it. Go over the bridge into Derbyshire and turn left. You are now on the main path through Dove Dale. However, according to the OS Outdoor Leisure map, this section is still Hall Dale, which seems a bit odd. The path soon swings right and climbs for a short distance to reach the Dove Holes, which are large water worn caves in the limestone crags to your right. The approach path can be slippery at times, so take care here, but also take time to do a bit of exploring. Continue along the path, which drops down to river level again. The route to the right leads up to Alsop en le Dale.

The signpost has been replaced. An earlier version had been broken so that the sign on one side read "Pub To Ale". Sublime optimism as there are no pubs in Alsop en le Dale.

Continue alongside the river. The crags on the other side of the river are known as Ravens' Tor, but one wonders when a raven was last seen there. Also, looking across the river you can see the alternative path – at least, you can when the river is not in spate, but when the water level is high some of the path is under water, so you made the right choice. The alternative route is definitely a high summer (and a dry summer) path.

Eventually the dale widens out somewhat and you reach Viator's Bridge. Go over the bridge into Milldale hamlet. This has such desirable facilities as toilets, a shelter a shop and a café. No pub unfortunately. The bridge is a classic packhorse structure and is very narrow. It is described in "Compleat Angler" as part of a journey from Ashbourne to Beresford Hall. The travellers had descended the steep side of Dove Dale by the packhorse route known as Hanson Toot. On seeing the route down and the bridge below, one of the travellers named in the book as "Viator") had

Ilam Rock

qualms about descending on horseback and described the bridge as "being but two fingers broad". Despite these misgivings, both travellers got down and across safely.

A short cut

If you've had enough at this point, or if time and the prospect of a visit to the George are more pressing, you can take a short cut from Milldale, back to Alstonefield. Instead of going along the lane beside the river, go left and immediately right, up Millway Lane. A steady pull up the lane (350 feet/107 metres of climbing in about a mile/1½ km) should bring you back into Alstonefield in about ½ hour.

Milldale to Coldeaton Bridge

Stroll along the lane beside the river. For the first few hundred yards/metres there's a riverside footpath, segregated from the road. For the rest of the way to Lode Mill there's a roadside footway. However, when the walk was recce'd the river level was so high that water was coming back through the road drains so the footway was impassable at some points. It wouldn't take much to flood this bit of road and when we saw how high the water had been a little further on the walk it was obvious that the lane must have been at least partly under water. Perhaps the Millway Lane option isn't such a bad idea after all.

As you approach Lode Mill there's a gate/stile on the left offering another short cut route up to Alstonefield. The emphasis is on the word "up". This is much steeper than Millway Lane.

At Lode Mill you join the Alstonefield-Alsop en le Dale road and bear right, over the bridge into Derbyshire again. This is the only point on the walk where you can reasonably deviate to catch a daily bus service back to Buxton or Ashbourne. The mill from which this settlement gets its name is on the Staffordshire bank and is in the process of being renovated.

Just over the bridge, go left, through a stile and down to the riverbank again. What follows is a delightful stroll in wonderful scenery, though it can be very wet underfoot after heavy rain.

The OS map shows that both side of the dale are open access, which makes the "Private. No access" signs on the two footbridges rather interesting. How else does one get to the west bank? No matter. Keep on the main east bank footpath until you reach Coldeaton Bridge. The bridge has a name plaque on the side so you can't mistake it. Also there's a sturdy brick and stone building beside it and a path leading off up to the right towards Alsop. However, you glance with apprehension at the west bank, for this is your route and it looks very steep.

Up Gipsy Bank to Alstonefield

Cross the bridge and begin the ascent of Gipsy Bank. You'll find that the path ascends the slope in a series of zig-zags. Clearly, some walkers have decided that these are too indirect and have ascended (or descended) in as near a straight line as possible, but this is folly. The zig-zags are much easier and you will be surprised how rapidly you gain height. Only near the top do the zig-zags give out and it is a wise course to make your own.

The sign at the top proclaims that this is National Trust land and that it is indeed Gipsy Bank, which is interesting, because the OS map show Gipsy Bank as being about 400 yards/370 metres upstream of this point. You'll almost certainly need to pause for breath here, and it's worth doing so, if only for the view down and across the dale. On the far horizon you'll be surprised to

Approaching Iron Tors

see a bridge. This is the former Ashbourne-Buxton railway line, now the Tissington Trail. The crags and wooded area just on the opposite side of the dale are known as Iron Tors. The prominent tuft of trees on the hilltop to the right is on Moat Low.

Duly rested, go over the stile into a narrow walled lane. This rises gently for a while and then Alstonefield church comes into view. The rest of the walk is a steady stroll, passing the Youth Hostel at Overdale and so reaching the road coming up from Lode Mill. Turn right here. 300 yards/275 metres should see you back at the village green and The George. Even after imbibing at The George you shouldn't need instructions how to get back to the car park and if you do you certainly shouldn't be driving!

Walk 2. Ashford in the Water

Route	Ashford, Sheldon, Magpie Mine, Sheldon (again), Great Shacklow Wood, Ashford Mill, Ashford
Distance	5½ miles (9¼ km). 1054 feet of ascent (321 metres). Allow 3 hours exclusive of stops
Grade	Moderate with one significant climb. The descent from Sheldon to Gt Shacklow Wood is steep and slippery in wet weather
Start	Bulls Head, Ashford. Map reference: 196697
Map	OS Explorer OL 24 The Peak District, White Peak Area
How to get there by bus	This is a 'well-bussed' village if we can coin such a phrase. There are daily buses from Bakewell, Buxton, Castleton, Chesterfield, Derby, Manchester, Matlock, and Stockport. High Peak TP is the main service. Some stop in the village near the church, others on the main road (A6), and others near the former Post Office. All are within a few minutes walk of the start
How to get there by car	From Chesterfield and Sheffield go to Baslow, then A619, and A6020 to Ashford. From Derby and the south follow A6 to Ashford. From Buxton, Manchester and the north-west follow A6 to Ashford. From The Potteries travel via Leek and Buxton and then via A6. There's a small car park near the Top Pump to the rear of the church

The Pubs

Cock and Pullet

In 1991, when this book was first published, the authors bemoaned the fact that Sheldon had lost its last pub, the celebrated Devonshire Arms. The only draught beer sold at this establishment was Inde Coope mild, drawn straight from the barrel into pot jugs. True aficionados would order a quart. Sadly, this classic hostelry closed in the early 1970s. Unusually, in the current era of pub closures, Sheldon has a pub again, the Cock and Pullet (01629 814292) opened to great applause in 1995. Step inside and you would imagine that this hostelry has been around for centuries – for there are artefacts and furniture that give the pub an air of longevity, not to mention the clocks. The fireplace is certainly a welcome sight for a frozen rambler – and it is only fair to warn you that the Magpie Mine site is not noted for its balmy climate. The new pub was (and still is), much welcomed by locals and walkers alike. The Cock and Pullet is open all day from 11am weekdays and 12 noon onwards on Sundays. It serves a variety of real ales, e.g. Hartington, Timothy Taylor's and a guest beer. Families are welcome. The pub has overnight accommodation and prides itself on serving good traditional food.

Bull's Head

On your return to Ashford you might also choose to call at the Bull's Head, a long-standing Robinson's pub situated near to the church. The Bull's Head stands back from the main street in the village. It has roses round the front door and seats outside, which are well liked on a sunny day in this sheltered alcove. If it were not for the cars parked in this tight space, the scene would be timeless, for in earlier times the Bull's Head was a coaching inn.

Relaxed walkers at the Bull's Head, Ashford

The pub has a very pleasant atmosphere and has been run by the same family for over 30 years. The bar on the left is the more usual haunt of ramblers. It is a cosy room with a roaring fire in winter. The other bar is larger and is more geared to food, which is on offer at lunchtimes. For the mud collectors amongst the walking fraternity the pub provides overshoes. Robinson's Unicorn and Old Stockport are available on hand pump.

Opening Times are; Weekdays 12 (11 Sat) - 3, 6 - 11, Sundays 12 - 3.30, 7 - 10.30.

The Walk

Leaving Ashford

From the front of the Bull's Head, turn right and walk to the corner just beyond the church. Turn left, passing a round, canopied seat and information board before crossing the Sheepwash Bridge over the River Wye. On the far bank you can see the pound where the sheep are held before being dipped in the river. The present bridge dates from the 17th century, but there were probably earlier bridges on the site.

Cross the A6 with great care and turn right. At the next junction, bear left along the lane signed to Sheldon. In a short distance, the lane bears left and at this point you go right, crossing a stile into a field alongside the river. The obvious riverside path is not your route however. Less than 100 yards/metres from the road go left, up the steep hillside. The path rises steadily, zig-zagging up the hillside, before bearing to the right and levelling somewhat as it reaches the corner of a drystone wall. Follow the wall uphill towards Little Shacklow Wood.

When you reach the corner of the wood, there's a well disguised stile in the wall. Negotiate this and carry on, up the field, bearing slightly left, away from the boundary of the wood. Go through a gap in the next field wall and on through the next field and another gap in the field wall, with the path now drawing closer to the wood again. Now the top of Magpie Mine chimney comes into view ahead. You'll see this at closer quarters later. The valley narrows as you draw nearer to Sheldon and you pass a mini sewage works below on your right. The path joins the road near a cottage at the eastern end of Sheldon village. If you have had enough or the temptation to call in the Cock and Pullet is irresistible, turn right at the road and head up the village until you reach the pub and there await your more dedicated colleagues, who will visit Magpie Mine first.

Magpie Mine

Turn right, along the road for about 160 yards (150 metres), passing Woodbine Farm on your left. Then go left, through a gate, passing a barn and with the wall to your right. The gaunt shape of the mine is now clearly in view on the skyline ahead of you. A series of stiles leads you across the little fields until a signpost points the way through a final squeezer stile and so into the field containing the mine (the mine-field?).

Magpie Mine was originally worked for lead, but latterly for fluorspar. There are around 20 shafts on the site and a number of buildings have been preserved here, including the "Cornish" engine house and the last version of the headgear. Further up the field, the Peak District Mines Historical Society has created a replica of a "horse-gin", the predecessor of the steam winding engine that resided in the massive engine house. Mining has taken place on this site from at least 1682 and Magpie was last worked in the 1950s but without much success. The mines here were difficult to work, accidents were frequent, murder not unknown and for very little return. The

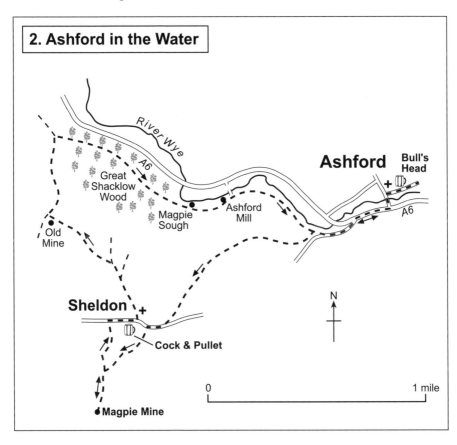

2. Ashford in the Water

most famous incident was the death of three Red Soil miners following a dispute over ownership of the various lead veins. Magpie miners used a technique known as "fire-setting" to break up the limestone rock. The resulting smoke and starvation of oxygen suffocated the Red Soil men. Despite the fact that "fire setting" should only have been carried out when warnings had been given and it was clear there were no miners in the vicinity (and neither of these had happened)no-one was ever charged with their deaths. No wonder that the mines are reputedly haunted. Quite what today's Health and Safety devotees would have made of this is interesting to speculate.

Having had a good (and careful) look around this fascinating site, retrace your steps across the field towards Sheldon and go through the stile whence you came. Sheldon is signposted at this point. Leave your earlier path and follow the signed route to Sheldon, passing through a series of little fields and soon emerging on the village street. It is possible to find at least three routes across these fields, but the choice is irrelevant as all go to the village. At the village street, locate the Cock and Pullet and any errant friends.

Sheldon to Great Shacklow Wood

NB. The descent from Sheldon to Gt Shacklow Wood is steep and slippery in wet weather. A possible alternative is to go via Deep Dale. This adds a mile (1½ km) and 135' (41 metres) of ascent to the walk. Deep Dale is a picture in spring when the orchids are in bloom and it is well worth using this route for that reason alone.

Head down the street from the pub towards the church and, near the church, go left along a narrow walled lane. As you leave the village behind, there's a good view to the north, over Tideslow and Longstone Edge to Mam Tor.

Ignore other narrow lanes leading off to the right and keep on this fine green lane as it descends. Keep your eyes peeled for a stile on the left about 540 yards (500 metres) from the church. Continuing on the green lane at this point will lead into difficulties – believe us.

Go through the stile and then through another on your right to enter a larger field. Carry on, now with the drystone wall to your left. The path now passes through a series of stiles and small fields, but is without navigational difficulties. The final stile in the series leads into a rough lane, by old lead mine workings. At the corner, leave the lane again and turn right, into a field – the path is signposted. In the next field, look for a stile on the left. This too is signposted. Cross the stile and make for the field corner where another signpost directs you to the right to descend to the wood.

At the edge of the wood, cross another gate/stile and begin the steep descent alongside the wall. This section can be very slippery so do take care. Part way down the hillside you come to a T-junction and here you turn right into Great Shacklow Wood.

Great Shacklow Wood to Ashford

The path is now much easier, though narrow. It is a delightful woodland walk, dropping gently at first, then more steeply as it gets closer to the bottom edge of the wood. The A6, which has betrayed its presence by traffic noise hitherto, can now be seen across the meadow and fishponds.

The path levels out as it passes the outfall of Magpie Sough.

A 'sough' is a drainage level and this one was driven to unwater Magpie Mine, which you visited earlier. The sough is around 1 mile (1.6 km) long. It took eight years to build and opened in 1881 at a cost of between £18,000 and £35,000. It is doubtful whether it ever really paid for itself. The collapse of an air shaft in the early 1960's led to an enormous build-up of water behind the blockage. The pressure build up caused a tremendous explosion in April 1966. Several hundred tons of shale and scree blew out of the shaft and partially blocked the River Wye. It didn't do the footpath any good either, but it did create an interesting physical feature. The water pressure was intense enough even then to form an obvious dome as it reached the top of the shaft and small stones thrown into the rising water came up again rather than sinking. In 1974, the sough was cleared and re-opened by members of the Peak District Mines Historical Society. The "new" outfall lies just to your left.

Continuing along the path you soon pass a partly restored water mill.

A lead smelter originally stood on this site, but latterly the mill was used for grinding corn. The smallest of the three wheels powered a pump, which supplied Sheldon with water.

Pass the mill and continue along the riverside path, a well-blazed highway. You soon reach the Sheldon road, and from here it is only a question of retracing your outward steps, back into Ashford village.

Walk 3. Ashover

The Route	Ashover, Fallgate, Gregory Mine, Overton, Goss Hall, Butts Quarry, Ashover
Distance	4 miles (6½ km). 700 feet of ascent (213 metres). Allow 2 to 2½ hours exclusive of stops
Grade	Moderate, with some climbs
Start	Ashover Village Hall car park. Map reference: 351633
Map	OS Explorer 269, Chesterfield and Alfreton
How to get there by bus	There are buses to Ashover from Chesterfield, Clay Cross and Matlock on Monday to Saturday(Hulleys 63/64). There are daily buses from Chesterfield and Matlock to Kelstedge (X17, Stagecoach), whence it is a pleasant walk along a bridle path to Ashover
How to get there by car	Take the A632 from Matlock or Chesterfield to Kelstedge and then the B6036 to Ashover. In the centre of the village turn left, passing the church and the Crispin public house. The car park is signed to the right by the Black Swan public house

The Pub

Old Poets Corner

It will be love at first sight for those who enjoy their real ale and good food for the Old Poets' Corner (tel: 01246 590888) prides itself in providing both. It is an unusual name for a pub, but poets do gather here for reading sessions at the regular poetry nights and then there are blues and folk evenings too. The beer menu is extensive, for the Old Poets has its own micro-brewery, (try Poets Tipple or Light Rale) as well as regularly featuring beers from other local micro and regional brewers, plus a selection of ciders.

On entering this hostelry you might possibly catch sight of the following: "Bread is the staff of life but Beer is life itself". That is no idle boast. The beer menu includes 'Ashover Gold' (brewed by The Leatherbritches brewery for the pub), 'Old Poets' (brewed by the Tower Brewery at Burton-upon-Trent) and a range of other beers, which often feature local micros and regional brewers. Add to this the bottled beers, plus the traditional ciders and perries, and you begin to realise that this is a rather special pub. In fact, one hot tip is to do the walking first.

The Old Poets Corner is open from 12 noon until 2.30pm and from 5pm on Mondays to Thursdays. It is open from 12 noon all day on Fridays, Saturdays and Sundays. Food is served every day from 12 noon until 2pm and from 6.30pm to 9pm (although in the busy season starts at 5.30pm). Sundays are different. There are carvery sittings at 12.30 and 1.45pm, then informally until approximately 3.30pm. Food is prepared fresh so you need to take this into account. Children are welcome in the dining room (no children in the bar as determined by law) and dogs are welcome. The landlord asks that walking groups 'phone beforehand so that long waits can be avoided. There's a website (www.oldpoets.co.uk) for the latest information and this will eventually include accommodation.

The last word is with the landlord who says: " We are a pub that serves food, not a restaurant that serves beer; walkers are always welcome at any time of the year".

Other pubs en route

Ashover village has two other pubs that you will encounter on this walk. They are; the Black Swan (01246 591926) and The Crispin (01246 5909110. Both are good pubs. Both serve a range of real ales and good food.

The Walk

Ashover

Ashover has been described as a microcosm of Derbyshire. The village is situated on limestone and surrounded by shales and gritstone - veritably a Peak District in miniature. In extent, it is one of the largest parishes in Derbyshire and within its boundaries at one time could be found coal and lead mines, foundries, mills and a wide diversity of agricultural practice, from moorland sheep farming to lowland arable farming. Now most of the industry has gone, but the village and the valley remain, arguably more delightful than ever. There's a maze of footpaths and a wealth of hostelries. This walk merely scratches the surface.

Ashover to Fall Hill

From the public car park by the village hall go left, into the village, passing the Black Swan on your right. Carry on towards the church, with its magnificent spire and, lo and behold, pub number two appears on the horizon.

The Crispin has one of the biggest inn signs in the county if not in the country. It tells the tale of the founding of the pub in 1417 following the Battle of Agincourt and then goes on to describe an incident in 1646 during the Civil War. Drunken Royalist soldiers ejected the landlord from the pub after he had tried to stop them drinking any more.

Immediately opposite the Crispin public house is the Institute. This is somewhat newer than the pub, only being built in 1860. There's an inscription over the door of the Institute, but it is in Latin and unlikely to be anything like as interesting as that of the pub opposite. For anyone seriously interested it is apparently a quotation from Proverbs XXII (6).

Ashover Church

At the Institute, go left, along a narrow path, which soon becomes a very narrow lane, with a wall on the left and a hedge on the right. This runs along the back of the playing fields and soon passes the pavilion. Continue straight ahead, through a series of stiles, with a wall close by, either on your right or your left. To your left there are views to the Fabrick; a gritstone outcrop perched on the rim of the Ashover valley. Also to your left you will see the ruins of Eastwood Hall, another casualty of the English Civil War. You soon emerge into an L-shaped field. Cross this and go through another stile, then follow the wall around the left-hand side of the field, down to a metal gate in the far corner.

Go through the squeezer stile by the gate and into a part of Fall Hill Wood, then emerging into a field again, only to plunge back into the wood. This area has been extensively worked for lead and fluorspar as the hillocks and hollows bear witness. On your right, the trees cease abruptly and there's the fenced cliff edge of Fall Hill Quarry. This is now disused and slowly re-vegetating, but keep well clear. The path winds through the wood with steep drops on either side. It soon descends to a metal post stile. Go right here, through a gateway, with a high stone wall to your left.

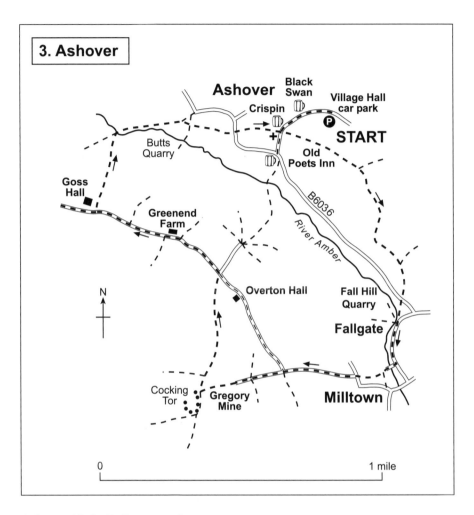

3. Ashover

Ashover Black Swan
Village Hall car park
Crispin
START
Butts Quarry
Old Poets Inn
Goss Hall
Greenend Farm
B6036
River Amber
N
Overton Hall
Fall Hill Quarry
Fallgate
Cocking Tor
Gregory Mine
Milltown
0
1 mile

Ashover Light Railway territory

Continuing along the path, you soon come right to the edge of Fall Hill Quarry, with its pool of blue water. Fortunately it is fenced off. To your left a new close-boarded fence hides a couple of substantial new houses on the site of what was once a fluorspar crushing plant. Go through a gap stile into a field and follow the right-hand boundary to another stile, where steps lead down to the B6036. At the time of the recce' there was a notice of a planning application to fill in Fall Hill Quarry with waste, so the description in the previous few sentences may soon be of historic interest only. Take great care crossing the road as there's neither verge nor footway and the road is narrow. Cross the road and go left, passing Ash Meadow and Greenbank House. Go down the drive of Greenbank House to locate a narrow path alongside the garage. The path was un-signed, but it is the route. The path descends quite sharply to cross a little stream by a stone slab bridge, before negotiating a squeezer stile and emerging on the road.

The road ahead leads to pub number three, in Milltown, but turn right and follow the bridleway sign, crossing the bridge over the Amber, to stand in the entrance to the former Milltown fluorspar washery, a place better known to narrow-gauge railway enthusiasts as Fallgate Yard.

Just over the bridge is the track-bed of the erstwhile Ashover Light Railway, opened shortly after the First World War. Although most of the line closed in the early 1950s, Fallgate lingered until the 1960s, with increasingly decrepit wagons being shunted over muddy rails between the washery and the lorry-loading ramp. Some rails are still in situ under the tarmac. The station building; a ramshackle affair of corrugated iron, still stands to the left of the bridge along with a solitary piece of track.

A well used but unsigned footpath leads alongside the river, round the back of the station building. The path is fenced off from the former washery site. The washery site itself has been landscaped and partitioned into smaller plots. At the next bridge, continue to follow the path beside the Amber, through the trees. The path swings right and forks. To the left lies the Miners' Arms. Take the right-hand fork, which soon crosses the former alignment of the railway. A short flight of steps follows, with a wall to the left and a fence to the right. Beyond the fence are the spoil heaps of the last mineral venture, this time for fluorspar. On the left, in a clump of trees, is a shaft, the remains of an 18th-century lead mine.

Overton Estate and Gregory Mine

Go over a stile and into fields. The path is fenced both sides, whether to stop walkers straying or protect them from savage beasts is difficult to say. You soon reach a rough lane.

(It is possible to cut the walk short at this point, by turning right, up a narrow track, which soon passes close to Overton Hall and thus reaches the top of Salters' Lane. A right turn down the field leads you directly to the Old Poets)

Continue ahead. Tree-clad hummocky ground on the right is again evidence of old lead and fluorspar workings. Where the trees end there's a view to Overton Hall. It was the purchase of the Overton Estate by the Clay Cross Company in 1918 that lead to the 20th-century exploitation of the mineral wealth of the valley, a process that has only recently ceased.

The lane continues, becoming increasingly rough and soon Cocking Tor is seen ahead, part of the gritstone fringe of this "Derbyshire in miniature". To the left, as you stroll along the road, is an area of rough ground, now being colonised by Scot's Pine. This area too was worked for lead and then fluorspar. Indeed, when this book was first published, in 1991, working had only recently ceased and the back-filled ground was far from stable.

The lane bears left towards Ravensnest Farm, then veers right to resume its ascent of the tor. Follow the lane past the remains of yet another fluorspar washery to the cottages, then go right, up a path, which rises sharply up the spoil banks of the fabled Gregory Mine. This mine worked underneath Cocking Tor, with the main drive leading towards Matlock. The westernmost working was the fore-field shaft at Old Engine Farm (map reference: 337617), the term "engine" relating to the winding engine. Lead mining in Ashover is recorded as early as the 15th century, but the heyday of Gregory Mine was in the 18th century when there were around 300 men at work. The mine finally closed in the first decade of the 19th century.

The path zigzags its way upwards, keeping to the right-hand side of the spoil heaps and with an unusual stone slab fence on your right. Reputedly, the stones were sourced from old pack-horse paving, but this doesn't seem

Cocking Tor from Ravensnest Lane

very likely as the stones show few, if any signs of wear. The prominent chimney to the left has nothing to do with the former mine.

Continue up the hill, soon joining a more prominent track where you bear right and shortly join another track, which slants across the tips. Go right here, but pause to admire the view back over Ashover Hay to Ogston Reservoir and to Hardwick Hall on the far horizon. The track now leaves the spoil heaps and plunges into the wood, over a device designed to stop motorcycle access.

Packhorse tracks

The track through the wood is wet in places and well-worn. It sees considerable use by horses, cyclists and motorcyclists as well as walkers. As the track emerges from the trees, you pass a stone trough on the left, whilst to the right is a view down to Overton "cottages" and Overton Hall. Where the path finally breaks free of the trees there's a fine stretch of raised stone causeway, parts of which are in sad need of repair. "Causey stones" indicate that this was once a well-used packhorse route. Proceed along what has now become a narrow lane, soon arriving at a crossroads. If you are feeling weary, or time is pressing, you can go straight ahead here, soon reaching a field path, which will take you quickly back to the centre of the village.

The route of the walk goes left at the crossroads and the track soon becomes a tarred lane. Another packhorse route joins from the right and the lane swings left, then right, to pass Greenend Farm. Continue along the lane, now passing Green House Farm on the left, at which point a fine view opens out over the upper valley of the Amber. Pass Overton Lodge on your right and continue along the now tree-lined lane until you reach Goss Hall. Just before the hall there's a stile on the right, giving out onto a curious stone walled ramp into a field. Head down the field, with the hall to your left. At the bottom of the field, pass through two stiles in quick succession, guarding an abandoned lane.

Descend across the next couple of fields, until, on your right you come alongside the start of a little valley with a small stream. The path passes through a gap in the wall and follows the course of the stream down to a gateway.

The Amber, Butts Quarry and so to Ashover

Descend still further, to a footbridge over the Amber. It is hard to believe that, back in 1816 there were serious proposals to canalise this river as part of a scheme to get Derbyshire lead via the Chesterfield Canal to the River Trent at Stockwith. Worries about water supply led to a railway proposal being substituted, but this never came to fruition until over 100 years later and then the line closed in 1951.

Once over the river, cross the motorcycle scrambles course twice and keep going down the valley, on a well-blazed track, parallel to the river. A bridge on the right gave access to Butts Quarry, once the mainstay of traffic on the Ashover Light Railway. It was the closure of this quarry that led to the demise of the line. Carry on alongside the river, ignoring the Butts Quarry bridge and a subsequent footbridge. Where the track swings left, go more or less straight on, through a little gate and then over a stream by means of a bridge. Ahead is a stile, approached by a stone slab bridge, beyond which the path twists and turns through scrub before emerging into a field. The course of the Ashover Light railway can be picked out as a low embankment on your right along with the remains of the bridge over the stream you have just crossed.

Keep to the left, heading up towards the electricity pole and soon the tip of Ashover church spire comes into view.

At the top of the bank you pass to the left of a house, through a gateway and onto a driveway leading down to the B6036. Cross the road and go left. After a short distance, just by Butts Grange, go through a squeezer stile on your right and follow this path towards the church. A final stile takes you onto a track between the churchyard and a house. If you are heading to the Old Poets, go along the track to the road and there turn right. The pub is about 150 yards (140 metres) away. Alternatively, if you are heading back to the car park, go up the flight of steps into the churchyard and follow the path which skirts round the left-hand side of the building. The church is dedicated to All Saints and is a beautiful building. At the western end there's an ancient stone coffin lid. Ashover was mentioned in Domesday as having a priest, church and mill.

You leave the churchyard by a gate that brings you out by the Crispin public house. Unless you are even more inebriated than the Royalist soldiers of 1646, you should be able to find your way back to the village hall from here without further description.

Walk 4. Brassington

The Route	Brassington village, Rainster Rocks, Longcliffe, High Peak Trail, Harboro' Rocks, Wirksworth Dale, Brassington village
Distance	4.7 miles (7.6 km). 843 feet of ascent (257 metres). Allow about 3 hours exclusive of stops
Grade	Moderate. Easy walking but there are some optional scrambling sections
Start	Wirksworth Dale car park and picnic site GR. 233547
Map	OS Explorer, OL 24. The Peak District, White Peak Area
How to get there by bus	There's a bus service (TM Travel 111/112) between Ashbourne and Matlock via Wirksworth on Mondays to Saturdays. There's a very handy stop in the village at the start of the walk
How to get there by car	Travel on the B5035 from Ashbourne and Cromford. Brassington is signed off this road. The car park and picnic site in Wirksworth Dale is signed up the minor road just on the northern outskirts of the village. You can park on street in the village, but space is very limited and thus it is not advisable. Indeed there are signs asking ramblers to use the car park and not park on-street

The Pubs

Brassington boasts two pubs, the Miners Arms or the Olde Gate Inn. Time was when it had no fewer than 17 such establishments. It must have been a drinker's paradise.

Ye Olde Gate

Ye Olde Gate (01629 540448) is an historic pub, built in the early 17th century. It takes its name from its position adjacent to the turnpike gate on the former main road. Legend has it that Bonnie Prince Charlie's soldiers were billeted here in 1745 on their ill-fated march to London, and apparently some of the oak beams may even have come from ships of the Spanish Armada. The pub is usually open from 12 noon until 2.30pm and from 6pm (7pm on Sundays).

There's an excellent pint of Marston's to be had, and Brakspear's beers are often on offer, plus good food, but please note that the pub requests that there are no children under 10 years of age. Ye Olde Gate has been named Britain's cosiest pub by The Times. It remains a real local pub, but is also very welcoming to visitors, including walkers. Closed Monday and Tuesday lunchtimes. No food served on Sunday evenings

The Miners' Arms

The Miners Arms (01629 540222)was first recorded in 1747 and is a popular traditional village pub, serving a range of well kept real ales as well as good value and locally sourced food. Whenever possible, 5 real ales are available, plus lagers, keg cider and traditional Somerset cider. Children are welcome and dogs are allowed. At one time it was the venue for the local Barmote Court, which dispensed lead mining law.

Opening Times: Weekdays, 12 - 2.30, 6 –11; Saturdays 12-3.30, 6-midnight; Sundays 12-4, 6 (8.30 in winter)–11. Closed all day Mon (except bank holidays), Tues lunchtime

The Walk

Into Brassington

From the car park and picnic site, go down the narrow lane to meet Dale End Road and there turn left. There's no footway on this road, so do take care. If you are making for one or other of Brassington's pubs at this stage, continue down Dale End until you reach the junction with Miners Hill and there turn right to find, first The Miners Arms and then, a little further on, beyond the church, The Olde Gate. (If, on the other hand, you are of the temperance persuasion or are delaying your imbibing until you've finished the walk, go to the next paragraph). On leaving the pub, make your way through the village to the nearby church of St James. The hillside behind the church rises so steeply that the church is almost built into the hillside. A path goes up through the churchyard to reach Hillside Lane and here you join your non-drinking companions (if any).

For the non-drinkers, turn right just past the village hall, up a little lane called Bowling Green. Follow this upwards until it reaches a T-junction and there turn left into Jaspers Lane. Almost at once, bear right, along Hillside Lane. It passes round the back of the church and from this vantage point you look down onto the church, which is built into the steep hillside. At the far end of the churchyard a footpath comes up from the main part of the village and here you will be joined by those who insisted on slaking their thirst at the start of the walk rather than at the end.

Continue along Hillside Lane to a stile just opposite Chapel House and here go right, into the fields. The path slants up across the field, wriggling its way through outcrops of limestone and overgrown lead mine spoil heaps. Where the path levels out, it is joined by another path coming up from the left and here you reach a stile. There's an extensive view southwards from here and ahead you can now see the impressive limestone outcrop of Rainster Rocks, your next objective.

The clearly defined path makes its way through more outcrops and spoil heaps and in this manner reaches a narrow walled lane. Once in the lane go left and descend for about 150 yards/metres to another stile on the right. Go over this into a large field, pockmarked with lead mine remains and with clear evidence of strip field agriculture. There are plenty of obvious paths, but most seem to be made by woolly cloven-footed walkers, not by booted hikers. However, Rainster Rocks are clearly in view ahead, so make a bee-line for these, avoiding the mine remains and passing to the right of a smaller rocky

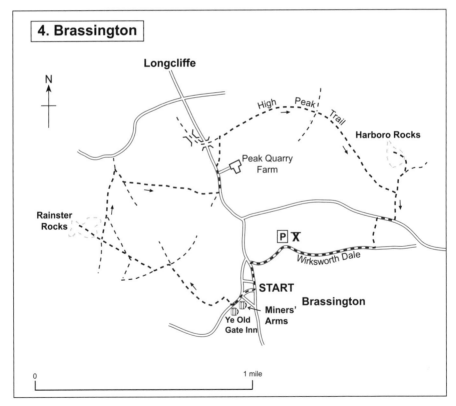

tor. Close to this smaller outcrop, you'll cross a broad track, but ignore this and continue ahead to a stile in the wall.

Rainster Rocks

Once over the stile, make for the waymarker post in the middle of the field and then go up the sketchy path to Rainster Rocks. This is an odd path because it only goes up to the rocks and no further. Where does it finish? That is not clear on the ground. Any semblance of a trodden route vanishes long before you reach the summit rocks and these can only be gained by a bit of scrambling, where you even have to use your hands! There are various comments on the Internet about access difficulties here, particularly for rock climbers. Some comments refer to there being a fence all round the rocks but there was no evidence of this on our recce' in February 2012. However, it is clear the rocks are NOT access land and what is more, THIS IS NOT A PLACE TO LET CHILDREN OFF THE LEASH. There are numerous clefts and rocks at odd angles, plus they are overgrown with moss etc.

Rainster Rocks was the site of a Romano-British settlement. This lay to the south-west of the main rock outcrop, again not on access land and in any case difficult to discern to the untrained eye.

Extricate yourself from the rocks, return to the waymarker post in mid-field and then turn left to reach a gate.

Once through the gate, follow the track up the field until you come to a sorry looking stone barn. Turn right here and go through a small gate, which is way marked. Skirt round to the right, following the boundary wall and thus locate another stile, which drops you into a narrow green lane. The lane ahead is not your route. Instead, turn left, through a gateway and into fields. Head straight up the field, making for a gateway in the middle of the wall. There's no obvious path, but as you approach the gateway, you'll see that it is waymarked with a large yellow disc – a useful confirmation that you are on the right route.

On either side of this field the bare bones of the limestone thrust through the thin soil, in sharp contrast to the field you are in.

In the next field repeat the process of heading straight on to a gateway, though this one is not waymarked. In the third field the path heads straight up the middle to a gap in the wall, just to the left of a small spoil heap. If you miss this, don't worry, because there's a gateway just to the left. The path, which is now more obvious, bears right to yet another gateway and there joins a bridleway. Bear left here, following the wall and so reach the Brassington-Longcliffe road.

Of dogs and railways

Turn left at the road, noting the curious red brick tower on the left hand hillside. Stroll along the road past Longcliffe Dale Farm and then, just opposite the Longcliffe boundary sign, there's a signposted stile on the right.

Ahead of you there's a bridge over the road. This carries the High Peak Trail, which was formerly the Cromford and High Peak Railway. This was a very early railway, opened in 1830 and using basically canal technology, with long level stretches, punctuated by steep rope worked inclines. Despite the incongruity of its operation, it had a remarkably long life, only closing in 1967. Longcliffe station can be seen away to the left.

Go over the stile and bear left to skirt the electricity sub station and the farm via a series of waymarked stiles. When the walk was recce'd the author was accompanied on this short section by three dogs from the farm. Their initial barking was a bit off-putting but they proved friendly enough. Having negotiated the various stiles (and dogs) you emerge on the High Peak Trail, overlooking Longcliffe works. Here turn right.

Bowl along the High Peak Trail, passing through some impressive limestone cuttings and over dry-stone embankments, marvelling at the construction of these with no more than picks and shovels in the early 19th century. As you emerge from one of these cuttings, Harbro' Rocks come into view ahead, crowned with a trig point. Immediately ahead is the industrial complex that is Hoben Minerals.

Harboro' Rocks and the High Peak Trail

As you approach Hoben Minerals you will notice on the hillside to your left, curious concrete structures. These are the remains of a crushing plant. At this point, according to the OS map, you are adjacent to access land, but, as in so many cases, you can't get onto it here. Instead, carry on along the Trail, passing Hoben Minerals until you reach a footpath crossing. Here go left, following the path signed to Grangemill. Ignoring the unfriendly notices, go up the hillside to the foot of Harbro' Rocks. The rocks rise in two tiers and there are various ways of getting up. These range from easy to downright dangerous. Just to the left of the path is a small ruined red brick building and behind it a large cave. This can be entered. At the back of the cave is a narrow tunnel leading into the hillside, but this is best left severely alone. Once out of the cave go back to the path and choose the easy route where the

Mystery structure, Harbro' Rocks

Harbro' Rocks

path is obvious rather than attempting to scale the rocks. The trig point on the summit is soon reached. There are superb views in all directions from here, reaching right into the heart of the Peak District looking north and southwards to Rugeley and Cannock Chase.

Retrace your steps to the High Peak Trail cross it, going down the track which skirts Hoben Minerals works and thus reach the road. Here you go right.

Brickworks and Dry Dales

Follow the road for about 325 yards (300 metres) Take care, for although this is not a heavily trafficked road, cars do come along at a fine speed and there's no footway and very little verge. Signs either side warn you not to trespass, but the look of the ground would deter most people anyway. Turn left at the footpath sign and go into a rough field, littered with hummocks and hollows that are clear indication of old lead mining. Keep to the wall on the left, skirting the quarry workings. Unusually, this is not a limestone quarry. Here clay and silica sands are being extracted for making refractory bricks. The clay is also used in the Wirksworth well dressings. The path follows the wall closely to avoid the lead spoil heaps and shafts, though the latter are all well and truly capped. The wall swings right and then left and the path follows it religiously, before descending to a gate and stile onto a narrow lane. To your left, the lane ends abruptly in a mound of spoil and a fence. This lane was once the main road into Brassington from Wirksworth but quarrying has severed it. The lane descends to Brassington down a narrow dry limestone dale, Wirksworth Dale, with some unusual views down into the village. After about ¼ mile (400 metres) you reach the picnic site and car park where, if you are a considerate soul you will have parked your car.

Time now for that pint you promised yourself some hours back.

Walk 5. Carsington

The Route	Carsington village, Sheepwash car park, Carsington Visitor Centre, Carsington Dam, Millfields, Upperfield Farm, Hall Wood, Hopton village, Carsington Village
Distance	8½ miles (13.7 km) 1044 feet of ascent (318 metres). Allow 3½ to 4 hours exclusive of stops. (You can add on a couple of hours for visits to the various bird hides, the visitor centre and the children's playground. Don't forget your binoculars!)
Grade	Moderate to hard. Easy walking, but quite long
Start	Miners Arms, Carsington. Map reference: 252533. Alternative start: Sheepwash car park, Carsington Water. Map reference: 248527
Map	OS Explorer, OL 24. The Peak District, White Peak Area
How to get there by bus	There's a daily bus service (TM Travel 110-112) between Ashbourne and Matlock via Wirksworth and there's a very handy stop in the village at the start of the walk
How to get there by car	Travel on the B5035 from Ashbourne and Cromford to the western end of Carsington by-pass. The Sheepwash car park is signed off to the right (from Ashbourne) and to the left (from Cromford). You can park in the village, but this is very limited and thus is not advisable. The Sheepwash car park is very popular (it's free) and can get very full early on

The Pub

Miners Arms

The Miners Arms at Carsington (tel: 01629 540207) is situated in the centre of the village, which has a long mining history. The pub is not immediately recognisable from the main street, but this limestone building has a rear entrance porch which leads into one main L-shaped bar. This area is divided into two with contemporary furniture for the most part, although there's a delightful room to the left of the main entrance given over as a dining area. The walls are adorned with pictures of Carsington reflecting the history of the village. Many people love to sit out in the sheltered garden in the warmer months and even in winter. As it is south facing it catches the sun through the afternoon and early evening.

The Miners Arms has three cask-conditioned beers on hand pull, usually including Draught Bass (brewed by the international combine Interbrew), a beer from the Black Sheep Brewery plus a changing guest beer. The usual opening times are 12 noon until 2.30pm on Mondays to Saturdays and from 7pm-10.30pm in the winter. On Sundays it is open 12 noon until 3.30pm and from 5pm until 9.30pm. In the summer the hours are extended until 3pm and 11pm weekdays and all day from 12 noon on Sundays. Food is usually served from 12 noon until 2.30pm and 7pm to 9pm (6pm start on Saturdays) on Monday to Saturdays. On Summer Sundays food is served all day until 8pm. Families are welcome.

The Walk

Carsington Village to Sheepwash car park

From the back of the Miners Arms, go up the narrow lane signposted as part of the Carsington Circular Walk. At the T junction, go straight on and the lane soon becomes a rough track. Follow this to the Carsington bypass road, which was built as part of the Carsington Reservoir project in the 1980's. Cross the road with care and turn right, immediately bearing left along the path signed for pedestrian use. The pedestrian and cycle routes round the reservoir are sometimes the same, sometimes segregated, but in the latter case the segregation is more honoured in the breach than the observance – and one cannot solely blame the cyclists for this either. The path dips to swing round an inlet and here for the first time you begin to catch a glimpse of the bird life that throngs this lake. At the top of the short rise there's a path to the first of the bird hides to your left. Anyone can go in and the only real request is that you keep quiet and don't disturb either the birds or people watching them.

After another short stretch there's a second path off to the left to another hide. Continuing ahead you then reach the Sheepwash car park.

Sheepwash to Visitor centre

Leave the Sheepwash car park by the path signed to the bombing tower and visitor centre. The path parallels a lane and there are glimpses of the lake to the left. On either side, in the fields there's evidence of ridge and furrow farming. Indeed, in the course of the construction of the reservoir and in subsequent investigations it has become obvious that the land hereabouts has been in continuous human occupation for well over 2000 years. After a short

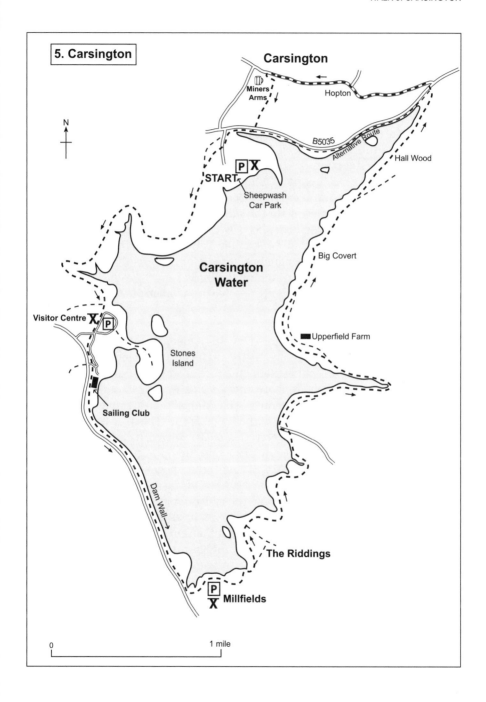

5. Carsington

Carsington

N

Miners
Arms

Hopton

B5035

Alternative Route

Hall Wood

START

Sheepwash
Car Park

**Carsington
Water**

Big Covert

Visitor Centre

Upperfield Farm

Stones
Island

Sailing Club

Dam Wall

The Riddings

Millfields

0   1 mile

distance you reach the bombing tower, an ugly red brick building with a staircase to the lookout area and with a clear view over the reservoir. The tower was originally constructed in the 1940's as part of a practice bombing range. Shortly, on your left, you pass the path leading to the Lane End Hide and a little while after that, there's a further hide on your right, beyond the cycle track.

The path emerges from a wooded area and you can see the visitor centre to your left. As the path swings right to skirt round an inlet, there's a good chance to use those binoculars, because there's nearly always a variety of waterfowl on this section of the reservoir. There's even a seat so you can observe in comfort. At this point the footpath and cycle path have become one, but the footpath soon veers way left and drops to cross a stream – there's a bridge, before climbing away up the other side of the inlet.

Note on your left the reed bed, specially constructed to attract a variety of bird species that require this sort of habitat. You now reach the Wildlife centre on your left and it is worth pausing here, if only to use the high quality binoculars and telescopes for watching the birds.

Continue along the path and you soon reach the main visitor centre.

Carsington Water Visitor Centre

The reservoir was formally opened by the Queen in May 1992 and not surprisingly has been a popular visitor attraction ever since. The Visitor Centre has an exhibition that explains the role of water in our daily lives. For those of you in need of sustenance there's a café and restaurant, plus the inevitable shops selling souvenirs. The shops are arranged around a courtyard, in the centre of which is the Kugel Stone. This is a 1 tonne ball of granite sitting on a thin film of water. Despite its weight, it can be moved with the touch of your hand! There's a fine children's playground close to the visitor centre, but many children will find the prospect of playing along the shoreline just as attractive.

Take the opportunity to walk along the causeway to Stones Island. Despite the name it isn't really an island so there's no risk of being cut off. On the island is a group of standing stones, reminiscent of the numerous stone circles that dot the Peak District landscape, but don't be fooled. These are new, having been commissioned by Severn Trent Water in 1992. The designer was Lewis Knight. The stones are all Derbyshire gritstone, ranging in height from 5½ to 13 feet (1.7 to 4 metres) and in weight up to 7.6 metric tonnes. You'll notice that some of the stones have holes drilled through them, some conveniently at child eye height. To children brought up on a diet of Dr. Who, Lord of the Rings and Harry Potter, these structures are a delight and many a fantasy game has been acted out here.

Carsington Water

Return to the Visitor Centre to continue the walk, or, if you've had enough at this stage, there's a daily bus service back to Carsington village. After this point there's no obvious short cut.

Visitor Centre to Millfields
Leave the visitor centre by the path signed to the Dam and Millfields. This passes to the right of the children's play area and the sailing club and so reaches the dam wall.

From the dam wall you get an almost full-length view up the reservoir to the hills at the back of Carsington. Planning approval has been given for a wind-farm on top of Carsington Pastures so the view will drastically alter. You can just see Harbro' Rocks overtopping Carsington Pastures. If you've a yen to visit these rocks, then try the Brassington walk in this book.

Stroll along the dam wall
Your eye will be drawn mainly to the reservoir and the various activities on it, but spare a glance down the valley towards the village of Hognaston, seen below. After a lot of dispute over the need for and location the reservoir, construction work commenced in 1979. The reservoir is part of a water compensation scheme, whereby water is pumped into the reservoir from the River Derwent, when that river is in full flow and vice versa when the river

level is low. A tunnel leads from the reservoir under the hill in front of you at the Millfields end of the dam. Construction of both the dam and the tunnel had problems. The dam wall collapsed, fortunately before there was any water in the reservoir, and work didn't recommence until 1984. The tunnel was originally to be bored and lined with concrete segments, but unsuspected geological conditions meant that this method couldn't be used and the concrete segments ended up being sold to various local businesses for retaining walls etc. When full, the reservoir holds 7,800 million gallons of water which makes it almost 25% bigger than Ladybower Reservoir (6,310 million gallons) and 90% bigger than the combined volumes of the other two Derwent Dams, Howden (1,980 m. gallons) and Derwent (2.120 m. gallons).

You soon reach Millfields. Here there's a specially constructed viewing area, plus a car park and toilets – but no bus service.

Millfields to the Hopton and Carsington by-pass

From Millfields car park follow the sign-posted path towards Carsington. If you were expecting this section of the round reservoir route to be less frequented than the earlier parts you'll be disappointed, but at least you can't get lost on this route – unless you do something very silly indeed. The path keeps close to the water, sometimes segregated from the cycle route, sometimes not, so be wary as few of the cyclists seem to have heard of giving "audible warning of approach" or even having such a simple device as a cycle bell on their machines.

The path briefly engages with Oldfield Lane where you go left and then almost immediately right. Oldfield Lane was one of a number of roads which was cut off by the construction of the reservoir and it is now a dead end. A short distance beyond Oldfield Lane you come across a small wooden building on your right. This is another children's fantasy dream. Inside there are big wooden chairs, a table and a fireplace into which you can squeeze. There's also a bat box and a nesting box because the front is always open so that birds and bats can get in and out. You'll have difficulty extracting the children from this place.

Continuing along the circular route, the path now swings into the biggest of the inlets. This has surprisingly steep sides and when the reservoir level is low, as it was when this walk was recce'd, you can really see the amount of draw-down, like a tide mark on the slope.

Much of the walk on this side of the reservoir is in woodland though never far from the water. When you do get a clear view, it takes in not only Stones Island and the visitor centre but also Carsington Pastures and the hills towards Brassington.

On now through Hall Wood, with a view across to Hopton Hall and so to the northern end of the reservoir, which is a paradise for reed loving birds. The path swings around the head of the reservoir and reaches the main road. This road was built as part of the reservoir construction project. It by-passes Hopton and Carsington villages and was specifically designed to ensure that construction traffic did not plough through the narrow village streets. Until recently, the circular route crossed the road at this point and then took a course through Hopton and Carsington villages, but now an off-road route has been constructed, running between the road and the reservoir and avoiding the double road crossing that was necessary hitherto.

Through Hopton and Carsington

However, as this walk is based around the Miners' Arms in Carsington you need to go on the old route, so cross the by-pass with care and go up the signed footpath to reach the village street. There turn left and enter Hopton. Although the village street has been by-passed, you need to take care because it is quite narrow and there's neither footway nor verge. Fortunately there'sn't much traffic either, though it is still the bus route. You soon pass the almshouses on your right. A plaque on the wall tells you that these were built at Philip Gell's behest to accommodate two men and two women. Construction began in 1719 and continued until 1722, which seems a long time for such a small building, but as Mr Gell had died in the meantime, perhaps it was this circumstance which delayed the work.

A short distance further on is a strange archway on your right. It has no apparent purpose. Still speculating on the reason for the arch, don't miss a rather fine milestone, which interestingly has the mileage to Alfreton on one face and an odd spelling of Ashbourne on the other. The road dips down to a junction and then bends left, alongside a high brick wall. It is best to walk on the right hand side of the road at this point, as the visibility round the bend is very poor. Keep on alongside the wall, which is part of the boundary of Hopton Hall. You'll soon see why it gets the name of the Crinkle Crankle Wall. This is a very unusual construction. The tower part way along the wall was originally a dovecote with a sort of summerhouse beneath. A short distance further on, beyond the brick wall, is the main entrance to Hopton Hall. Although the hall is not open to the public, the gardens and grounds are usually open during the snowdrop season and they are well worth a visit. You also get a fine view of the frontage of the hall on these occasions and, like the Crinkle Crankle Wall, it is quite an unusual design.

A few yards beyond Hopton Hall a boundary stone on your right shows you have passed from Hopton township into Carsington township. The Miners' Arms can now be seen ahead, so you should have no further need of description.

Walk 6. Chelmorton

The Route	Chelmorton village, Pomeroy, Flagg, Town Head
Distance	5.6 miles (9 km). 650 feet of ascent (198 metres). Allow 2½ to 3 hours exclusive of stops
Grade	Moderate with some gradual climbs
Start	The Church Inn, Chelmorton. Map reference: 114703
Map	OS Explorer OL24 The Peak District, White Peak Area
How to get there by bus	There's a bus, (Hulley's 177) to the village of Chelmorton from Bakewell and Buxton on Mondays to Saturdays. This is infrequent service although the morning trip out of Buxton and back works well. Do not despair, however, as there's a regular daily High Peak service TP from Buxton and Derby and Nottingham. This calls at the end of a lane by Chelmorton. From here there's a pleasant 10-minute walk to the village of Chelmorton – about half a mile at most. Some may prefer to catch the 42/42A High Peak bus from Ashbourne and Buxton, which stops near to the Duke of York at Pomeroy and start the walk there instead. This service operates daily but the Sunday service is limited; however the High Peak 58 also serves Pomeroy on Sundays and Bank Holidays
How to get there by car	Travel on the A515 Ashbourne to Buxton road and turn into the A5270 at Brierlow Bar. If travelling via the A6, turn onto the A5270 at the top of Topley Pike hill. Chelmorton is signposted from the A5270. On-street car parking is available but please park with consideration

The Pubs

Church Inn

The Church Inn at Chelmorton (tel: 01298 85319) is appropriately named for it stands on higher ground opposite the church at the head of the village. The pub is set back from the left-hand side of the main street and at 1260 feet above sea level (388 metres) it is one of the highest pubs in the Peak District.

There are seats outside to rest awhile and these make it an idyllic location on a summer's day. Inside, the main bar is given over to dining, but there's still a pub atmosphere and be assured the walker is always welcome whatever the season. In winter the fire is a real attraction. At the bar there are three cask beers on offer from the Adnam's and Marston's breweries. There's often a guest beer too.

The Church Inn is open from 12 noon until 3pm and from 6.30pm to 11pm in the evenings every day of the week. Food is served from 12 noon until 2.30pm and from 6.30pm until 8.30pm daily and families are welcome. There's overnight accommodation for those who wish to stay in the area.

Duke of York

You will also pass by the Duke of York at Pomeroy, a Robinson's roadside house with extensive gardens and a camping/caravan site behind. The building was originally a farm in the 15th century but in the early 17th century it was converted to a coaching inn to serve the growing trade on the road from Buxton to London. This continued as Buxton became more popular as a place to take the waters in the next century. This all came to an end with the arrival of the railways in the 19th century but the inn has continued to welcome passers-by since those heady days. The pub openly welcomes walkers but asks you to clean up your boots on the scraper provided. There's a main lounge bar and this has a roaring fire on a winter's day. There's also an unusual feature on the wall, a list of all the landlords and landladies that have served here since 1618. That's some achievement. The inn prides itself on its locally sourced home-made food. The Duke is open all day. Make it a two-stop walk!

The Walk

Chelmorton

The village is mediaeval in shape with one main road running through a line of limestone houses and farms. Little tracks lead off to strips of land peeling away from the dwellings. These ancient strip fields are now fossilised by drystone walls and offer a distinct character to the area. In reality, the narrow walled fields are some of the finest examples in the country. This early farming community owes its existence to a spring, the Illy Willy water, which rises alongside the lane just above the church and has been channelled through the village before disappearing down a swallow hole. Worth a look. Also, before you start the walk, take a look at the church (not the pub). Look at the weathervane and whilst you are going on the walk try to work out what type of insect it represents. Then, when you've found that out, use that knowledge

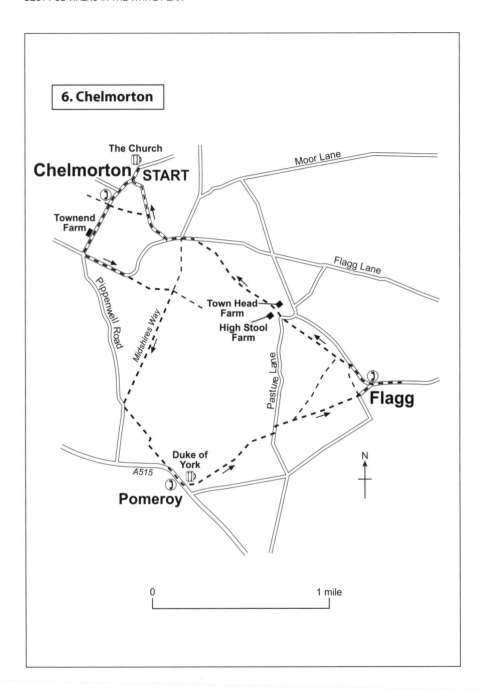

to work out to which saint the church is dedicated. Here endeth the RE exam.

Start the walk from the Church Inn at Chelmorton and go down the road through the village.

Walk the entire length of the main street until a crossroads is reached. This is the site of the mediaeval town ditch and you'll catch sight of the old pound as well as the village water channels. Cross the road and turn left to walk facing the traffic. At the left hand bend, go over a stone step stile into the field and head up the hillside to cross another stile. Proceed slightly right again to cross another two stiles. Keep ahead, with the drystone wall on your right and then turn right to walk along the wide track.

Illy Willy Water, Chelmorton

Pomeroy

This rough track is part of the Midshires Way, which as the name suggests, offers a multi-user trail for the most part, through middle England. The track eventually gives out onto a lane, which has the delightful name of Pippenwell Road.

For those who want to cut the walk short you can turn right here and it will lead back to the crossroads at Chelmorton. Otherwise, turn left almost immediately and go over a stone step stile to enter a field. Keep ahead, following the drystone wall on the right. Cross a stile and continue ahead to go over another boundary wall before crossing a stile near to the electricity pole (pylon). Walk over to the opposite field boundary and then turn left, ignoring the stile in this wall. At this point you are following the alignment of the Buxton-Derby Roman road. Go through the gateway and walk to the corner of the field where a stile exits onto the main road, the A515. From here, the A515 is also on the alignment of the Roman road at this point and this is indicated by the Street Farm place name given to the farm on your right.

Turn left to walk the short distance on the road verge to the Duke of York pub at Pomeroy. Thankfully it is a short stretch. Along the main road to the right is a boundary stone marking the different quarters of the Hartington townships or parishes. Be careful hereabouts because the traffic travels at speed – the Romans knew what they were doing when they laid out this road! Just beyond the pub car park you will find a stile on the left. Cross it and head for the stone stile in the wall opposite. Walk across the next field to the left, aiming for a stile approximately half way down. In the next field, head across to the far corner, where two stiles are crossed in succession. Head for a gateway located in the far wall and in the direction of a small spinney. Go over the step stile and walk by the compound through the next field, then follow the drystone wall on your left to exit onto a lane.

Flagg

Turn left on this narrow lane, but not for long. As it begins to rise, go right, over a stile to enter a field. Follow the boundary wall ahead, then crossing one stone stile and through a squeeze stile, then a gap stile, before reaching a barred gate that leads into a lane near Flagg. Once on the road, turn left and follow it to a junction, where the 177 bus stops, and village information is displayed. Flagg is one of the quietest rural communities in this part of the Peak District, but all that changes during the few days around the point-to-point races when thousands come to watch the event. There's no pub here now so most people make their way to the Duke at Pomeroy. Turn left at the junction and walk past the nursery school on the left and houses on the right. Look for the finger post on the left and cross the stile here to enter the field.

Head 45 degrees right, then cross a step stile and proceed ahead to another by a group of trees. Continue in a similar direction; you need to cross a couple of step stiles to the left of two gateways. There's a band of trees to the left and High Stool Farm. Go ahead to meet the road by the entrance to High Stool Farm. Two paths are signposted at the farm. Your way is right of the farm entrance through a wicket gate, past two old gateposts. Ease around to the right of the mound with the walled woodland ahead. Townhead Farm is to the right. Go over the next stile to the left of a gateway on the left and your way is slightly right, across to a stone stile located in the middle of the wall. Head slightly left to another stone stile. Go over another stile and continue towards a solitary tree. There's a stile just to the left of it.

Bear slightly left away from the drystone wall, climbing over the bank towards the far-left corner. Here the road is joined.

Fine Views

The steady climb is almost over and, to be frank, it can be a bit of a trudge when the ground is wet. Go left and walk facing the traffic. Take the second turning right. This lane runs above the village of Chelmorton, with fine views of the village and the strip enclosures. There's a chance to walk through them as part way down this narrow hillside road, after the bend, is a finger post on the left. This is your way. Go through the gap stile and drop down to a gateway. This leads to a drive and it is necessary to follow this to the main street of Chelmorton. Turn right for the Church Inn.

If time (and energy) permit, it is worth going beyond the pub to see the source of the village water supply and then ascending Chelmorton Low. At over 1450 feet (446 metres) this is a superb viewpoint and well worth the climb. It is access land and the summit contains the remains of Bronze Age burial mounds.

Walk 7. Darley Bridge

The Route	Darley Bridge, Oker Hill, Snitterton, Ash Plantation, Wensley, Oldfield Lane, and Darley Bridge
Distance	5.1 miles (8¼ km). 1016 feet of ascent (310 metres). Allow 2½ to 3 hours exclusive of stops, but including ascent of Oker Hill
Grade	Moderate to hard, with opportunity to omit some climbing if desired
Start	Darley Bridge picnic site. Map reference: 270624
Map	OS Explorer OL24 The Peak District, White Peak Area
How to get there by bus	There's a Monday to Saturday service to the starting point from Matlock and Bakewell. There's a daily service to Whitworth (Darley Dale), on the Trent 'TP' from Derby, Manchester, Nottingham, Stockport, Buxton, Bakewell and Matlock; it is a 15-minute walk from here to Darley Bridge
How to get there by car	From A6 follow B5057 (signed to Winster). Go over the level crossing and the crossroads. The car park is about 220 yards (200 metres) further on
How to get there by train	Darley Dale station is served by Peak Rail's trains from Matlock and Northwood. Hopefully during the currency of this book the Matlock-Derby branch trains will be extended to serve Darley Dale and Rowsley

The Pub

Square and Compass

The Square and Compass at Darley Bridge is a Robinson's house. (01629 733255). It was, and apparently still is, the furthest east pub owned by this company and was the subject of some disagreement in the Robinson family when it was first acquired. It has two bars, both fortunately with tiled floors, but this has more to do with the propensity of the nearby river to flood than the need to accommodate muddy booted walkers. However, such visitors are warmly welcomed, and for added pleasure there's a lovely roaring fire in wintertime. Food is served lunchtimes and evenings and there's a fine range of Robinson's beers on offer, including Old Tom – but this is only sold in halves. The standard of insult from certain members of the bar staff is delightfully high.

The Walk

Darley Bridge

From the car park, go right, along the B5057 road towards the Square and Compass Inn, passing the entrance to the Darley Dale Cricket Club, which was founded in 1863. The curious wall on the far side of the road was designed to keep cattle in, but let floodwater through. It works! Pass the pub – far too early in the walk for partaking of liquid refreshment, and go over the fine old bridge. Note that all the arches on this north side are round. On the far side of the bridge, turn left, along the lane signed to Oaker (gated road). Oaker or Oker? The county highways department prefers the former; locals and the OS prefer the latter. Now note the arches on this southern side of the bridge. They are pointed, usually a sign of mediaeval origins. Mediaeval bridges were normally built with pointed arches, but the upstream sides were most prone to flood damage and consequent rebuilding in more "modern" styles, hence the round arches. Darley Bridge has suffered flood damage repeatedly over the years and has also been widened on the upstream side as well.

The Oker road sees little traffic and in any case you are only on it for about 100yards/metres before going right, over a stile and into fields. A clear path heads diagonally across the field, heading towards the prominent tree on top of Oker Hill. The field betrays evidence of former ridge and furrow farming. The furrows are invariably wet. Leave this field by a stile and then keep up the right-hand side of the next field, passing a barn to your left, before reaching a rough lane.

At this point you have a choice, whether or not to ascend Oker Hill. The route of the walk does include the ascent, but it can be avoided. If you wish to avoid the ascent, read on. Otherwise, skip the next three paragraphs.

Avoiding Oker Hill

At the rough lane go left. Follow the lane down past the houses. Beyond this point the lane becomes no more than a grassy track. At the first gate past the houses, bear right along a narrow path, leaving the hedge and track to your left and beginning to skirt Oker Hill. The route is waymarked and obvious underfoot. The tumbled nature of the ground hereabouts is evidence of

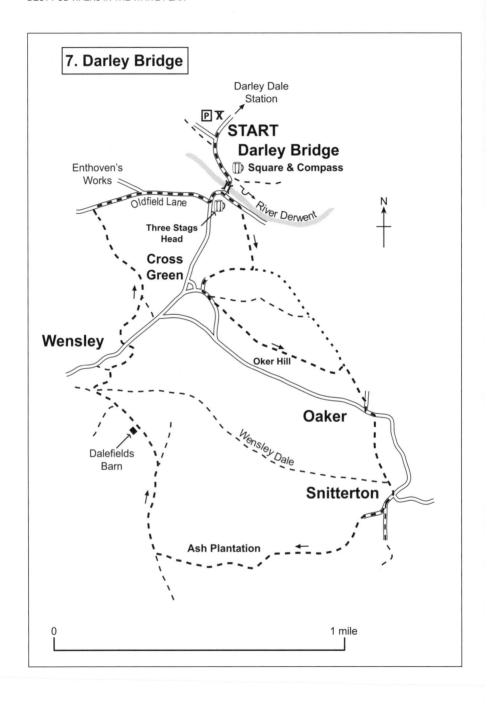

7. Darley Bridge

Darley Dale
Station

START
Darley Bridge

Square & Compass

Enthoven's
Works

Oldfield Lane

River Derwent

N

Three Stags
Head

Cross
Green

Wensley

Oker Hill

Oaker

Dalefields
Barn

Wensley Dale

Snitterton

Ash Plantation

0   1 mile

landslip, for Oker Hill is composed of shales and grits; a notoriously unstable combination.

Follow the path upwards. At the first stile there's a fine view down the valley towards Matlock and Riber Castle. As you continue to climb the view is more constricted, for there's a thick growth of scrub, but eventually you break free of this to gain open hillside. Head for the curious pointed object, which looks like the tip of a buried church steeple, but which turns out to be a local version of a fence post. When this ramble was first being walked, there was a curious feeling of walking in a time warp. The walk was accompanied at regular intervals by the sound of passing steam trains and then to cap it all an aeroplane that looked like a survivor of the First World War made a series of passes around the hill. Only a farmer in a smock and leading a carthorse was missing from the scene.

Descend slightly towards a derelict barn and pick up a clear cart track. At Grace's Well (a spring in a small walled enclosure on the left) there's a way mark which points up onto the shoulder of Oker Hill. The official walk route rejoins at this point.

Grace's Well, Oker

Ascent of Oker Hill

If you're a summit bagger, go right at the rough lane. After only a few yards there's a stile on your left and a well-blazed path heads off up the field. The stile and path are unsigned and the path doesn't appear on the map so your right to use it is uncertain. A pity because it offers a near direct ascent route of the hill. In the circumstances, it is better to carry on along the lane until you reach the road at Cross Green and there turn left. After only a few yards there's another lane on your left, and immediately ahead a gate and stile leading onto the north ridge of Oker Hill. This is a permissive path. It ascends steeply (and muddily) to reach the trig point that marks the summit of this miniature mountain at 627 feet (193 metres). The view from here is excellent and well worth the climb. Carry on along the ridge, which is surprisingly narrow. If this were another 2000 feet higher we would be talking razor edge ridges and risks of vertigo. You go through a stile on which there's a notice explaining about the permissive

Robin on Oker Hill

path and why this hill is of ecological interest and just beyond this is the prominent tree you saw right at the start of the walk.

This is Will Shore's tree. The legend is that the two Shore brothers said their last goodbyes on this spot, each planting a tree before they departed. One tree alone now flourishes, though it must be doubtful whether it is the original version. Wordsworth put the legend into verse in 1829.

Having admired the view, continue along the ridge, descending now through thorn scrub on what can be a very muddy and slippery path until you come out into the open again and reach a waymark post. Go left here and descend to join the wimps' route that avoided the hill. Note on your left the spring in the small walled enclosure. This is Grace's Well, which was apparently named after a Grace Greatorex. The well used to supply water to the local cottages, prior to the installation of mains water.

On to Snitterton

When you reach the track by Grace's Well, turn right and at once seek out a stile on the left. This leads into a patch of scrub, but the way through is clear enough though slippery in wet weather, and you soon come into a field. Cross the field, making for the gate in the far corner. There you'll find a stile. Go over the stile into the lane and then go right, to the T-junction. In less than 100 yards/metres, there's a stile on the right and a footpath heads off towards Snitterton. Keep the hedge on your left, pass through a gateway and then across a bridge spanning the Wensleydale Brook. Straight on now, heading for the left-hand top corner of the field, where there's a signpost. Go through the gate and follow the path to what looks like a garden gate, but which in fact is the entrance to a narrow ginnel between a house and a bungalow. This leads into the Bull Ring in the centre of Snitterton.

Don't panic, the Bull Ring only relates to an iron ring set in the road. A plaque proclaims that it is indeed the Bull Ring, but doesn't tell you anything else. Depending on which tale you hear, the ring was for tethering bulls that were being baited or were being tied there to wait patiently for cows to be brought to them for "servicing".

Go right on emerging from the ginnel and head up the lane marked with the "No through road" sign,

Snitterton Bull Ring

leading towards Snitterton Hall. Ignore the footpath sign pointing up the drive to Leawood Farm and continue along the lane, which now bears right, passing the hall. This is a fine Elizabethan building, surrounded by a high stone wall and with its own Home Farm alongside. When this walk was being recce'd the current owners of the hall were having an underground swimming pool constructed and it was possible to see into the excavation. Almost certainly this is the biggest building project in Snitterton for many a long year. The lane ends at the farm entrance and a notice proclaims that access is "By appointment only" and that you "Enter at your own risk". Despite this welcome, carry on past the sign and skirt round the left-hand side of the farm to where a track goes off up the hillside, through a gate, passing a new(ish) house en route.

An exercise in route finding

Follow this track upwards to the next gate, which has no stile, but which opens readily once you've worked out how to do it. Leave the track at this point and bear right along the waymarked hollow-way. Follow this upwards, beside the wall until you reach a stile. Go straight on to the waymark and then bear left through a gap in the wall. At this point all semblance of a path ceases and you find yourself in a rough field. Make your way across the field as best you can, eventually spotting another waymark, half hidden by a tree. There's the suggestion of a terrace here, leading to a ruined building, which you pass. At the wall, bear left and follow this up hill to a stile. Cross the field, heading up hill and bearing left to a stile in the far top corner of the field. All these are waymarked, a great improvement of when this walk was first included in this book. Here at last the path becomes distinct as it weaves through the wood and out into open fields again.

Continue along the path, which soon swings left alongside the electricity line. To the left is Tearsall Mine, originally a lead mine but more recently worked for fluorspar. At the junction of paths, go right, and descend to a stile in the corner of the field, passing more old mine workings on the way. The path you are now on was the miners' path from Bonsall to Millclose Mine. When this walk was recce'd recently a party of cavers was just about to descend one of the shafts closest to the path. This is marked with a steel shaft cover and leads into Tearsall Pipe Mine. The path has the great virtue of being waymarked and obvious underfoot, pursuing an unerring course between the various lead mine shafts as it skirts round the head of Northern Dale. Wherever there might be possible confusion there are waymark posts, but after the third stile the path does become indistinct. Follow the wall on your left to reach the beginnings of a track after which there's no difficulty in route finding. Wensley village soon comes into view.

Wensley

Stroll past the monumental Dalefields Barn, now sadly neglected and falling into ruin. The track then drops into the head of Wensleydale, describes a graceful arc and climbs out up the opposite side. Here you reach a tarmac road by the first houses of Wensley village. Where the road swings left into the Square, you go right, through a stile, then down a paved path to reach the main road close to Wensley Hall.

On the opposite side of the road is a footpath sign to Stanton and Birchover. The path starts up the driveway to a house, skirts round to the right of it and then bears right as a narrow green lane. This soon enters fields and continues as a broad grassy track to a gate. Just before this point there's a stile on the right. Go over this and into a large field. Here the path bears slightly left, making for a stile about halfway down the left-hand side. The approaches to this stile are frequently "damp". Once through the stile bear right and head for the far right-hand corner of the field, there entering the wood.

Enthoven's Wood

You are now on a broad forest ride between conifers. Follow the ride, which soon begins to descend quite sharply and bears left. The track then forks and there's a waymark indicating paths straight ahead and to the right. Take the right hand track, which zigzags steeply down to the stream. Another path crosses here, but keep on the main track, which climbs away from the brook and then bears left by what appears to be a eucalyptus tree. The plantation through which you are now passing was planted to screen Enthoven's works. Enthoven's is on the site of the famous Millclose Mine, probably Derbyshire's most successful lead-mining venture, which only ceased operation in the 1940s. There are occasional notices that proclaim that the woodland is private and that there are security patrols active, so it is not clear whether you are allowed to use the various paths that venture into the trees. Instead, carry on along the track and so arrive at Oldfield Lane. Turn right here for a steady stroll down the road, back to Darley Bridge. Take care, as there's no footway or verge and lorries to and from Enthoven's use the road.

At Darley Bridge you join the B5057, almost opposite the Three Stags Heads; an almost irresistible temptation, though it was closed on the recent recce, then it's back over the Derwent, pausing for refreshment at the Square and Compass before finally reaching the car park, the station or the bus stops.

Walk 8. Earl Sterndale

The Route	**Earl Sterndale, Harley Grange, Dowel Dale, Booth Farm, The Fough, Hollinsclough, Glutton Bridge, Earl Sterndale**
Distance	**5.4 miles (8.6 km). 1002 feet of ascent (305 metres). Allow about 3 hours exclusive of stops**
Grade	**Moderate with a few climbs. (Rather more serious if you decide to go up Parkhouse Hill)**
Start	**The Quiet Woman, Earl Sterndale. Map reference: 090670**
Map	**OS Explorer OL 24. The Peak District, White Peak Area**
How to get there by bus	**There's a daily bus service High Peak 442 between Ashbourne and Buxton. This runs approximately every two hours. The bus stops opposite the bus shelter near the pub for Buxton and at the shelter for Ashbourne**
How to get there by car	**Travel on the B5053 from Brierlow Bar near Buxton or from Bottom House near Leek. The turning to Earl Sterndale is signed from this road. The only parking is on street and is very limited**

The Pub

The Quiet Woman

The Quiet Woman at Earl Sterndale (tel: 01298 83211) is an unpretentious Peak District pub not given over to food but focusing on good hospitality for both locals and visitors. The name is unusual and the inn sign includes the words 'Soft Words Turneth Away Wrath' referring to the tale of an earlier landlord who chopped off his wife's head to stop her ranting at him all night and day. The gory pub sign illustrates the fact. Evidently, the villagers at the time happened to be one hundred percent behind his rather desperate action.

The main room is the bar and, whilst there has been ongoing upkeep, this has been undertaken in a sympathetic manner including the restoration of natural beams. The open fire in winter is a real plus for the walker – and the settles and wooden tables make this a place to get comfortable. This is especially the case on Sundays when folk music is sometimes played.

There are Marston's beers on hand pull and often a guest beer on tap too. Food (mainly light snacks) is available including marvellous pork pies produced in the Buxton area. The Quiet Woman is usually open at lunchtimes from 12 noon until 3.00pm and from 7pm in the evening daily. On the bar local produce is often for sale, including free-range eggs and cheese. There's also camping in the field behind the pub. Thus, in summary, this is a very good place to adjourn after any walk. Across the road and village green is the church, the only rural church to be the target, unintended we assume, of a bomb in the Second World War. In true British spirit, a wedding, due to take place the following day, did so in the ruined chancel.

The Walk

From the entrance to the Quiet Woman, turn left on the road and follow this as it descends to a crossroads at the head of Glutton Dale. Cross over the main road and walk ahead on a minor road. This climbs up past dwellings and then levels and bends to the right. About 700 yards from the cross-roads, (625 metres), look out for a path leading off left, as there's no finger post. You cut left through a gate and head slightly right across the field to join a track. Cross the track and a wooden stile.

Dowel Dale

Immediately, you need to go left to climb up the field, keeping company with the wall on the left and thus parallel with the track. Cross a stile where a footpath sign points the way to Dowel Dale. Walk ahead across the field and lo and behold the scenic splendour of the dale comes into view. Go through a gate and now it is eyes down, for the path plunges down the valley side to another gate and exits onto the road. Turn right to walk up the dale, a bit of a climb but the stillness of the valley occupies the mind as you make your way onwards and upwards. The road then sweeps to the right on open ground and then curves to the left by the entrance track to Greensides Farm, which lies to your right.

Follow the road upwards, passing over a cattle grid, thus reaching an isolated junction where you go left. This road also rises to a cattle grid, gateway and stile. Once through, your way is to the right, waymarked to Booth Farm. Keep ahead through a broken down wall then you should catch an unusual view of the roof of Stoop Farm below to your left. You encounter another broken wall and from here you'll need to proceed ahead, crossing two stiles before joining the road. Go left towards Booth Farm.

When the road begins to bend right for the farm, keep ahead on a track. This cuts through a gateway and then descends along the edge of a beautiful valley nestled in the lee of Hollins Hill.

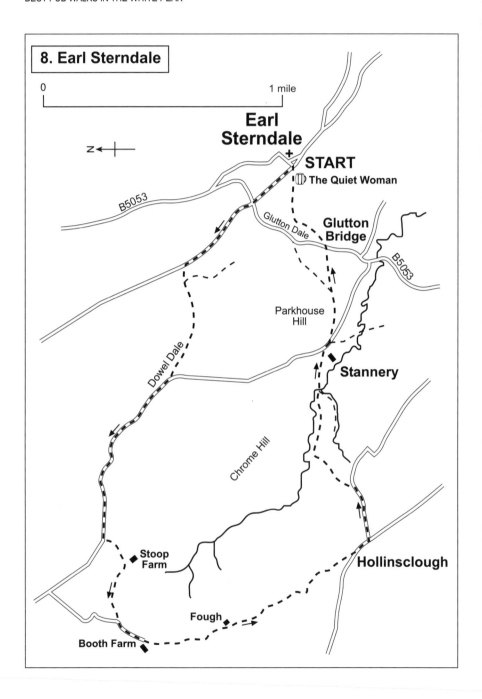

8. Earl Sterndale

0   1 mile

Earl
Sterndale
START
The Quiet Woman

B5053

Glutton Dale

Glutton
Bridge

B5053

Parkhouse
Hill

Dowel Dale

Stannery

Chrome Hill

Stoop
Farm

Hollinsclough

Fough

Booth Farm

The track passes to the left of a house known as The Fough and continues ahead to a fork. Take the lower track into the valley bottom. Cross a step stile by a barred gate.

Pause awhile as there are superb views of Chrome and Parkhouse hills here. Are these two the reason why the Peak District is thus named? No, of course not but they do looks like Peaks and now form an Site of Special Scientific Interest given their reef limestone geology and the associated flora.

Anyway, before the corner, as the track follows the hillside towards Hollins Farm, drop down to the stream where you cross a packhorse bridge over the infant Dove, thus leaving Derbyshire and entering Staffordshire.

Hollinsclough

The path now climbs the hillside, slightly left, up to and following a drystone wall. This leads to a road where you turn left into the isolated hamlet of Hollinsclough.

Here is a classic example of the loss of amenity in rural settlements for there's no longer a post office, shop, school or pub here and it rarely sees a bus.

Pass the Bethel chapel dating from 1801, built by local jaggerman, John Lomas.

A jaggerman was responsible for leading teams of packhorses through the Peak District and the trough which used to be situated here would have been to refresh the packhorses at this point.

Turn left at the junction to walk by the old school and church, dating from the 1840s, and leave the hamlet.

The road leaves the settlement, bends left and then right at a corner where you'll spot a track on the left after a cattle grid. That is your way. Continue ahead on the track through fields. Proceed through a gateway on the right and over the footbridge by the ford. Now keep ahead towards the gateway near to Stannery Farm. Go through a small gate and turn right on the road where you will see a stile on the right. Your way is now slightly left across a large pasture towards a stone marker mid-way across.

To your left rise the mighty Chrome and Parkhouse hills, designated as open access land after many years of being forbidden territory. If you've a yearning to climb Parkhouse Hill you'll need to go left on reaching the road. After about 300 yards/metres make your way up the NW ridge of Parkhouse. After a sharp, steep climb and an exhilarating "stroll" along the narrow crest, you'll eventually descend to Glutton Grange and the B5053, where you turn right to reach the path referred to in the next but one paragraph.

Continue along the path to a stile by a barred gate and keep straight on here. Go over a stream. The gate in the wall ahead is marked in yellow and exits onto the B5053.

Cross the road and go through the gate into this lower part of Glutton Dale, a name which may well be associated with naughty eating habits. That is one to ponder over as you climb, climb and climb out of the dale. Head slightly left up and across the field to go through a stone gap stile. The path then turns left and becomes a steep climb as it curves right and then left to a stile near the brow. Look back at the view. It is worth the climb. Walk ahead to another gap stile by a gateway and then go slightly right across a field now heading in the direction of Earl Sterndale church. This well-worn path leads through a couple of small enclosures and behind a cottage to exit by the Quiet Woman public house. It is possibly time for some tea or something a little stronger.

Walk 9. Great Longstone

The Route	Great Longstone, Hardrake Lane, Longstone Edge, Moor Lane, Little Longstone, Monsal Head, Fin Cop, Little Lane, Thornbridge, Great Longstone
Distance	8 miles (12.9 km). 1384 feet of ascent (422 metres). Allow 4 to 4½ of hours exclusive of stops. (Shorter options available)
Grade	Moderate. Easy walking with only one climb of any note up to the edge.
Start	The White Lion in Gt. Longstone. Map reference: 199718
Map	OS Explorer OL24 The Peak District, White Peak Area
How to get there by bus	There's a daily service from Bakewell, Castleton and Tideswell to Great Longstone, Little Longstone and Monsal Head (Hulleys 173)
How to get there by car	Travel on the A6020 from Ashford in The Water and turn left as signed. There's very limited car parking in the village so please be considerate. There's a small lay-by in Little Longstone close to the Packhorse and there's a 150 space car park (pay and display) at Monsal Head. Any of these would do

Four pubs and a massacre

This is a lengthy walk but it has some superb views, especially from Fin Cop and along Longstone Edge. It would be easy to take short cuts and these are mentioned in the text. It is the only walk in this book that features FOUR pubs en route and it's certainly the only one that visits the site of a massacre.

The pubs

The four pubs on this route are; the White Lion and the Crispin in Great Longstone, the Packhorse in Little Longstone and the Monsal Head Hotel at Monsal Head of course. The description of the Monsal Head Hotel is given in Walk 16, where it is also the featured pub.

It is rather unusual that one village has two pubs owned by the same brewery but in the village of Great Longstone this is clearly the case. Robinson's offer both The Crispin and The White Lion public houses and within a stone's throw of each other. Both of these hostelries welcome the walker.

The White Lion

The White Lion (tel: 01629 640252) has a number of benches outside and between these there are steps up to the main entrance to enter this friendly two-roomed pub; the tap bar and lounge/dining area. There's a warming open fire in winter. The pub serves cask-conditioned beers from the Robinson's range. The range, by the way, includes Hatters Light Mild, Old Stockport Bitter, Best Bitter, Double Hop and Old Tom in addition to seasonal beers. Obviously, only some of the range is available at any given time.

The White Lion is open 12 noon until 3pm and 6pm onwards (5.30pm in summer). Food is usually available from 12 noon until 2pm and from 6pm until 8.30pm (2.30pm and 9pm at weekends). There's a tapas menu available until 10pm. Please note that the pub is closed on Tuesdays – so if you are standing outside a very quiet pub, check the day. Families are welcome and dogs are allowed in the tap bar only. Groups of ramblers are advised to book in advance. The pub has a large car park to the rear and it may be possible to arrange with the landlord to park there while you do the walk, assuming of course that you are going to patronise the pub when you return.

The Crispin

This traditional pub (tel: 01629 640237) has an emphasis on good value food and has been described as a "gastro" pub by some. Somehow the idea of Derbyshire oatcakes (a pub speciality) and the notion of a "gastro" pub don't quite match. There's a good drinks choice too, with usually four of Robinson's beers on hand pump, to say nothing of the wines and whiskies. Bar food times are from 12-2.30 and 6.30-9.

Opening Times are: Weekdays 12 - 3, 6 - midnight; Saturday and Sunday 12 – midnight.

The Packhorse

The Packhorse (01629 640471) is a fine little pub, which has been sitting prettily in the hamlet of Little Longstone in very much the same way for the past two hundred years or so. As its name suggests it most likely existed to serve the jaggers (the men who led the packhorse trains) on this turnpike route out of Chesterfield to Wardlow Mires.

There are two bars and a small dining room. The pub serves hand-pulled beers from Thornbridge and Theakston's breweries and also Moravka, a Czech style lager brewed at the Taddington Brewery, Blackwell.

The garden area is ideal for children and the Packhorse is well known for its exceptional bar food. Families are welcome (well-behaved children) but cannot, by law, be in the tap bar. Walkers with or without muddy boots or

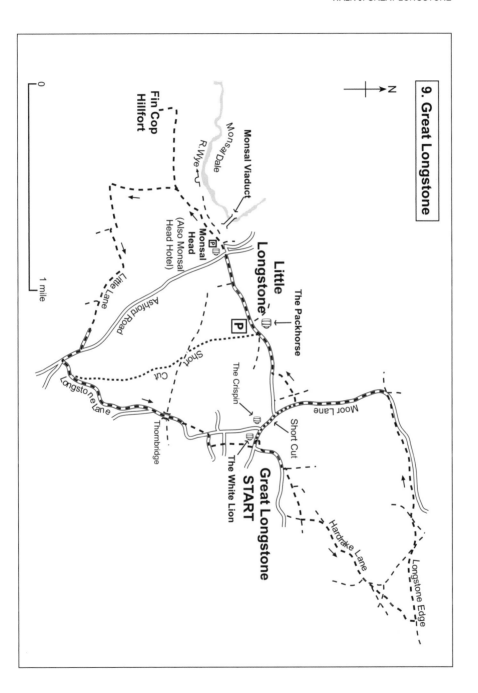

9. Great Longstone

N

0

1 mile

Fin Cop
Hillfort

Monsal Dale

R. Wye

Monsal Viaduct

Monsal
Head
(Also Monsal
Head Hotel)

Ashford Road

Little Lane

Little
Longstone

The Packhorse

P

Short Cut

Longstone Lane

The Crispin

Thornbridge

Moor Lane

Short Cut

Great Longstone
START

The White Lion

Hardrake Lane

Longstone Edge

dogs are welcome in either bar. With some justification this pub is regarded as one of the best in the Peak District.

The pub is open from 12 - 3pm and from 5pm in the evening on Monday to Fridays. It is open all day at the weekends. Food is served from 12noon until 2pm and from 6pm - 8.30pm every day.

The Walk

Leaving Great Longstone

Great Longstone is one of the more traditional of the Peakland villages and does not suffer from an excess of visitors. The houses nestled around the village green are mainly of stone but Longstone Hall stands out as a red brick structure of considerable character. Besides the mining and quarrying on the nearby edge and farming this area was also at one time a centre for stocking manufacture. Not that there's much evidence left to signify this.

From The White Lion go left, then before the village green and bus shelter, turn right between houses opposite the school. The way is signposted to the church up a narrow lane. Turn right part way up, through a kissing gate on a path to the churchyard. Another kissing gate takes you into the churchyard. If you have time take a look inside the church, which is dedicated to St. Giles, the patron saint of cripples, beggars and blacksmiths. Gt. Longstone church is one of a large number of medieval foundations dedicated to St Giles. Indeed there were originally eight such dedications in Derbyshire alone. In the Middle Ages his cult was especially popular in poor rural areas, but little is known about the man himself. Legend has it that he lived as a hermit in southern France in the eighth century. There he rescued a deer being hunted by Flavius Wamba, king of the Visigoths. This action so impressed the king that he established a monastery and Giles became the abbot.

Continue ahead through the churchyard to a stile out onto a lane. Go along the lane and just beyond a large dwelling on the left, go left along a track, signed as a footpath. After about 50 yards/metres go right, along another walled track. In about 150 yards/metres, where this track swings left, go straight on through a stile and into fields. Follow the path straight ahead through a couple of fields and over a farm track until your reach a step stile, which drops you into another walled lane. This is Hardrake Lane and here you turn left.

Onto Longstone Edge

Stroll up Hardrake Lane, which is a no more than a narrow walled track. The track gradually gains height and Longstone Edge can be seen to your left. The lane curves up through a shallow valley and soon reaches the rake from which it gets its name. The hummocks and hollows on your left are obvious signs of old lead mining. Don't explore too closely! At this point, the lane finishes and you are confronted by a bewildering series of little gates and signs. Straight ahead of you is a farm track, fenced on the left. There's a footpath gate in this, though quite why isn't entirely clear. A short way along the track, there's another gate in the fence and a Peak and Northern Footpaths Society sign, giving very clear directions. Your route is the one described as "Coombs Dale via Bleaklow". Don't panic, the Bleaklow referred to here is not the 2000 foot massif north of Kinder Scout. Leave the track, go through the gate and bear left towards another little gate. As you approach this gate, you'll realise that there's no fence joining it on the right, so it's useless. Passing the gate, do not head for the stile in the wall ahead, but bear right, making for the top right hand corner of the field. There you'll find a well-hidden stile and gate, which takes you onto the access land of Longstone Edge. Continue up the hillside. The lower slopes of the Edge are covered in thorn scrub, but the path is obvious underfoot and without difficulty. The path tops a rise by two large trees. Here go left along a broad cleared area with no obvious path. However, in about 100 yards/metres you join a track, which runs unerringly along the flanks of Longstone Edge, with tremendous views to the left. Pause to take in the view across to the Wye and Derwent valleys and even over to Magpie Mine near Sheldon, featured in the Ashford walk. Fin Cop, the Iron Age hill fort that you will visit later, is also in view ahead.

The broad track continues, more or less level until it meets a path coming up from the left. Here the track forks. Ignore the track to the right and carry straight on, descending slightly to reach a gate and stile. Beyond the stile carry on up the track, ignoring the path, which bears away to the left. Down to your left you can see the humps and hollows of the Hard Rake lead workings and the little known Stanshill Dale leading back towards Gt. Longstone. The track you are on is also the result of mining activity, but of a much later period. The old lead miner sank shafts up on top of Longstone Edge and used the steep slope of the edge as a convenient tip for mine waste. 20th century mineral working valued this waste, which contained fluorspar and barytes so much of the waste was scraped off the slope leaving the original land surface exposed. You can still make out the earlier tipped surface where mature trees and electricity poles have been left in situ on raised mounds of spoil. Quite odd.

The track ends abruptly at a mound of earth, but a path skirts to the left of this to reach Moor Lane, just by the cattle grid. Go down the lane, which soon swings left, passing an old loading dock. There was once a winding incline here for bringing minerals down from the Watersaw mines on the top of the

Edge to carts. Such a system was commonplace in the North Wales slate quarries, but unusual in Derbyshire.

Decision time

Continue down the lane until you reach a signpost indicating a "byway open to all traffic". This is decision time. You can cut the walk in half here by simply carrying on down the lane for about 350 yards (325 metres) to Great Longstone. The Crispin and the White Lion will then be within spitting distance. Alternatively, turn right here and soon pass Dale Farm on your right. Just beyond the farm, there's a stile. Go over this and then through a series of fields, eventually passing between a house on the left and a ruined barn on your right. Just beyond the house, go left, over a stile and down a track to the road. Turn right and stroll down the road into Little Longstone, passing Little Longstone Manor on your right. There's no footway at first, so do take care. As you arrive in Little Longstone, the Packhorse Inn is on your right. You could of course finish your walk here as well. The same bus service links both Great and Little Longstone and, if you've parked in Great Longstone you have only to retrace your steps from the Packhorse for about 100 yards/metres and there's a path to your right across the fields, which will take you back to the village. Make sure you take the correct path otherwise you'll end up on the Monsal Trail!

Onwards to Fin Cop

From the Packhorse, carry on up the road to Monsal Head. There's a footway along this section. Between Little Longstone and Monsal Head seems to be a popular bit of road for people wanting to avoid Derbyshire Dales District Council's exorbitant car park charges. It gets solidly parked up very early, especially at weekends. Little Longstone chapel lies to your right and a lovely little building it is. The chapel is open during daylight hours. Visitors are welcome.

At Monsal Head, cross the main road, to the short stay car park. The view from the short stay car park is one of the classics of the Peak District. It would have been radically different if late 19th century railway promoters had had their way. Another viaduct would have graced the scene, stretching from the crags on the right hand side of the dale over to the hillside towards Brushfield. The viaduct would have been almost 300 feet (91.4 metres) above river level and would certainly have dominated the view. Resist the blandishments of the Stables Bar and go through a stile just where the road swings right. Turn left, following the signpost to Ashford and Monsal Dale. Almost at once the path forks and here you go left following the signs for Ashford. The path is narrow and keeps an almost level course along the top of the dale, with occasional views down into the depths and across to Brushfield Hough. For most of the year, the view (and any sense of exposure), will be hidden by trees. Eventually you reach a clearing, where there's a seat and another signpost for Ashford. Ahead you can see the profile of Fin Cop and looking down the slope you can make out the rocky outcrop known as Hob's House. All this slope is now access land. You could cut out the trip to Fin Cop and carry on along the path to Ashford, but that would deprive you of a superb view.

Continue along the dale top, on a narrow path, hemmed in by a wall on the left and an increasingly steep slope on your right. No sense of exposure as the trees and scrub come right up to the path. Over the wall you get a glimpse of the earth ramparts of Fin Cop hill fort. The path reaches a fence, in which there's a stile. Go over the stile onto open hillside, obviously grazed by cattle. The fort is immediately on your left, but does not form part of access land. Continue to the wall corner and stand here for a moment to admire the view, which is very extensive. The land falls away very steeply ahead of you and to the right. Obviously a fine defensive situation, but not good enough. Recent archaeological digs have uncovered evidence of a massacre in the early 4th century. The remains of 9 women and children have been found beneath the collapsed ruins of the fortress wall. As the archaeological dig has only looked at a small portion of the site so far, there may well be others to be found. Evidence also suggests that there was human settlement on this site for close on a thousand years prior to the massacre. Further details can be found on the Longstone Local History web site

Retrace your steps back to the junction with the Ashford path and then turn right.

Little Lane and Longstone

The way ahead is along a narrow walled lane. You emerge from this into open fields, but retain a wall on the left. Just past a dewpond on the left, there's a gate and stile. Go left here and follow the field wall down to twin gates in the bottom right hand corner. Go through a stile by the right hand gate and into another narrow walled lane. This is Pennyunk Lane, but you are only in this for about 100 yard/metres before reaching a junction. Go left into Greengate Lane, a name which describes the track beautifully. Go down Greengate Lane, which soon makes a right-angled turn to pass through Finlea farm complex, changing names at it does so to Little Lane. Beyond this point the lane is obviously well used by farm vehicles, but their use ceases at another set of twin gates, where Little Lane continues straight ahead and here obviously only used by pedestrians. In this manner you have descended gently from the heights of Fin Cop and are now approaching Ashford. Parkfield House is just to your left, a fine ecclesiastical looking building.

Beyond this you now reach Ashford Lane, the B6465 and here go right, keeping to the verge on the right hand side. Follow the main road down to its junction with Vicarage Lane and Longstone Lane. Cross the B6465 and go along Longstone Lane.

Who was Lord Marples?

The rest of the walk scarcely needs description because you can follow this road all the way back to Great Longstone. However, there are one or two things to look out for en route.

The first is about 540 yards (500 metres) from the junction with the B6465. Here a path goes off left, signposted to Little Longstone. If you have parked at Little Longstone or Monsal Head and want to cut the walk short, this is where you do it. Go left here and follow the well-blazed path up to and across the Monsal Trail to emerge almost opposite The Packhorse in Little Longstone.

The second point of interest is Thornbridge Hall, the buildings of which are on both side of the road and very fine they are too. This is of particular interest to beer aficionados, because this is the spiritual home of Thornbridge brewery, though the brewery itself is now located in Bakewell.

The third point of interest is a sad reminder of the erstwhile Minister of Transport and it lies a little further on, when you cross the bridge spanning the Monsal Trail. To the left is the former Great Longstone station, for this was once a main line from Derby to Manchester and a victim of the machinations of the infamous Beeching cuts of the late 1960's. You can blame Ernest Marples for bringing in Beeching in the first place, but you can't blame him for agreeing to the closure proposal. That dreadful deed rests with Barbara Castle. Great Longstone station had an interesting shadow life before it finally closed. Although regular passenger trains had ceased to call there on 10/9/1962, apparently one train in each direction stopped there on weekdays to pick up a district nurse who worked in Buxton. No-one else was allowed to board or alight, which seems ridiculous, but that was British Railways for you. This arrangement persisted until the final withdrawal of local passenger services in 1967.

Just beyond the station, the lane bends to the right and a footpath takes off through a stile on the left, crossing the field and cutting off the road corner. The path re-emerges onto the road close to the 30mph signs. Turn right into Glebe Avenue and keep your eyes peeled for a ginnel on the left. It is unsigned but is just before you reach the next road junction. Go along this ginnel, cross another road into another ginnel, which soon reaches the recreation ground.

Keep straight on alongside the recreation ground, at the far end of which you come to a car park. This turns out to belong to the White Lion. Leaving the car park to your left you'll find another narrow ginnel. This drops you down beside the pub and lands you safely on the main street of Great Longstone.

Great Longstone Station

Walk 10. Hulme End

The Route	Hulme End Visitor Centre, Brund Mill, Sheen, Townend, and Hulme End
Distance	4½ miles (7¼ km). 385 feet of ascent (118 metres). Allow 2½ to 3 hours exclusive of stops
Grade	Easy
Start	Visitor Centre, Hulme End. Map reference: 104593
Map	OS Explorer OL24 The Peak District, White Peak Area
How to get there by bus	There's a daily bus service, High Peak 442, between Ashbourne and Buxton via Hartington and Hulme End. The demand responsive service, Moorlands Connect serves Hulme End on Mondays to Saturdays, telephone 0300 1118003 for details
How to get there by car	Travel on the B5054 from Newhaven on the A515 or from Bottom House on the B5053 to Warslow then right for Hulme End

The Pub

The Manifold Inn (nee The Light Railway)

The Manifold Inn at Hulme End (tel: 01298 84537) is a handsome stone building set back from the road at the junction to Alstonefield and by the bridge over the River Manifold where an old toll house still stands. The origins of the inn almost certainly date back to coaching days, but with the arrival of the metal tracks in the valley, it became known as the Light Railway, an association with the Leek and Manifold Light Railway, which brought thousands of visitors to the area in earlier times. The railway closed in 1934, but it took 50 years for the name change to occur, much to the annoyance of pub historians and railway enthusiasts alike.

On entering the inn, there are old photographs of cricket teams and a brass band. Step ahead a few paces and there's a small reception area, a dining room to the right, a conservatory room to the rear and a spacious lounge bar to the left. There are usually three real ales on offer, including local brews such as

Hartington Bitter brewed at Whim Brewery located at a farm not many miles away, so it really is locally sourced. Other beers include offerings from the Titanic Brewery located in the Potteries and much loved in north Staffordshire. There's also a real interest in the provision of good food and the inn prides its home-cooked daily specials. There's also private camping site behind the pub for those who fancy staying in the area.

The Manifold Inn is open 12 noon until 3pm and from 6pm on Monday to Thursdays and all day on Fridays through to Sundays. Food is served from 12 noon until 2pm and from 6.30 to 8.30 daily. Families are welcome as are dogs. The bus for Buxton stops outside and the stop for Hartington and Ashbourne is on the other side near to the old tollhouse – so it could not be more convenient.

The Walk

Hulme End (for Sheen and Hartington)

The visitor centre is located in the former station building. The station name board proclaims that this is Hulme End (For Sheen and Hartington). Like many stations it was miles away from places it purported to serve. The railway opened in 1904 and closed in 1934. Following the closure, the trackbed was purchased by Staffordshire County Council and converted into a footpath. The station at Hulme End became a highways department depot and served

Miniature railway at Hulme End (1984. 50th anniversary of closure of L&MLR)

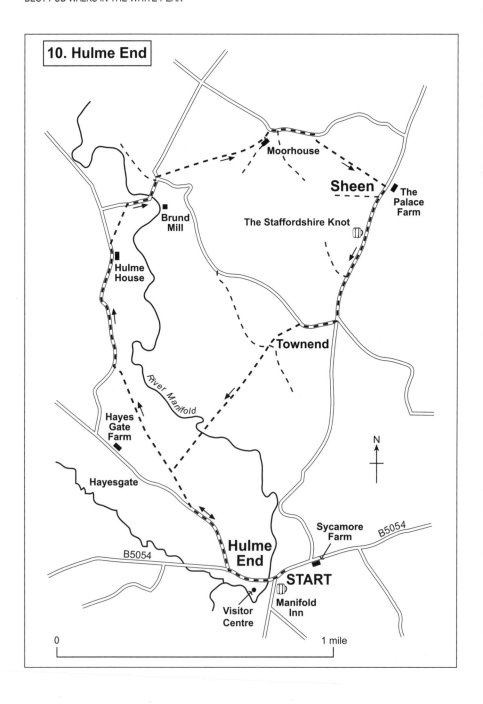

10. Hulme End

Moorhouse

Sheen
The Palace Farm

Brund Mill

The Staffordshire Knot

Hulme House

Townend

River Manifold

Hayes Gate Farm

Hayesgate

N

Sycamore Farm

B5054

Hulme End

B5054

START

Manifold Inn

Visitor Centre

0   1 mile

as such for many years. When the highways department moved out there was sufficient interest in the old buildings to ensure their survival and restoration. It was commendable effort in our view, thanks to the tenacity of the Staffordshire Moorlands Tourism Officer at the time.

Leave the visitor centre at Hulme End to join the B5054 but please take extreme care when crossing the road for traffic emerges from the bend faster than safe driving would dictate. Go right and proceed for approximately 30 yards/metres to reach a junction beyond the small chapel dating from 1834. Go left here and walk along this quiet lane towards Hayesgate Farm. However, before reaching the farm look on the right for a finger post and small gate. Pass through this to enter the field and walk ahead to go through another small gate. Now keep company with the fence on the right, and proceed through another gate. The farm buildings lie to your left as you continue straight ahead (and not through the gate on the right) to a small gate and then to a stile. Follow the old hedge line and through the gap at the end, identified by the old stone gateposts. The last section of path leads to a stile and a road.

Brund

Go right and walk along the lane towards Longnor. There are good views of Sheen Hill ahead. After about 600 yards/metres you pass Hulme House Farm. By the finger post go through a gate on the right, into a meadow. Head diagonally across the field, then go through a gate to join a road again. Go right here; walk over the bridge spanning the River Manifold, which at one time powered a mill complex at this small hamlet known as Brund.

Climb to the junction (avoiding the stile on the right beforehand) and before you is a stile signposted to Sheen. Enter the field and head very slightly right, up through a succession of small fields and passing over four stone step stiles. Go through a gap stile, then keep ahead towards Moorhouse Farm, with a drystone wall to your right. You might also catch a glimpse of Sheen church on the right. Just past the farm there's a gap stile on the right. Once through this, turn left to the drive and through a gap stile by the barred gate, which leads to a road.

Go right here, ignoring the first signpost on the right. After about 300 yards/metres you approach the bend when the road dips. Cross a stile on the right by the waymarker post.

Now gather your bearings and head left up the hillside towards a fine group of trees at the top of the hill. You reach a field corner and a last climb leads up to a gateway on the brow of this little ridge. There's a stone step stile to the right of the gateway and once over keep ahead. Do not be tempted to focus on the signpost; this happens to mark a path leading off in the opposite direction from the road. You will see your stile just to the left of this as you get closer.

Sheen

The path emerges onto the road in Sheen, a windswept moorland village clustered around its church. It is amazing that it still hosts an inn, the Staffordshire Knot, which focuses on good food but also has a small bar area. There's also a youth hostel in the village. Go right on the road and pass by the Knot. Follow the road, known here as Pown Street, to a crossroads at a location known as Townend. Go right at this junction and pass the Belle Engineering factory. As the road bends at the bottom of the works, go left along a track that soon leads into a field ahead. Cross a gap stile by a barred gate. Continue ahead and follow the drystone wall down into the valley passing a small paddock and a dwelling known as Buttsend. Go through a gap stile, then straight ahead across the flood plain, keeping near to the wall on the right and thus reaching a footbridge over the meandering Manifold.

Walk ahead through a water meadow. Here you can see evidence of abandoned meanders and this is bound to dredge up memories of your old geography lessons. Cross the gap stile by the barred gate and rise up the bank. There are no clear landmarks at first but then Hayesgate Farm comes into sight once more. Keep ahead and go through the small gate in the next boundary. Turn immediately left and retrace your steps along this outward stretch of path to the road where you turn left for Hulme End again.

When you reach the main road (B5054), the Visitor Centre lies a few paces to the right, but the way to the Manifold Inn is to the left. There's also a handy village shop, which sells light refreshments so it is a good place all round to enjoy a post-walk tipple or tea.

Walk 11. Litton

The Route	Litton, Tansley Dale, optional ascents of Wardlow Hay Cop and Peter's Stone, Cressbrook Dale, Ravensdale, Cressbrook, Litton Mill, Tideswell Dale, Litton Dale, Litton
Distance	Basic route 5.1 miles (8.1 km). 1261 feet of ascent (384 metres). Allow 2½ to 3 hours exclusive of stops. The ascent of Wardlow Hay Cop adds 1.3 miles (2.1 km) and 450 feet (137 metres) of ascent. A trip to Peter's Stone adds 0.9 miles (1.5 km) and 365 feet (111 metres) of ascent. To do the full route would involve 7.3 miles (11.75 km) and 2076 feet (633 metres) of ascent and would require 4 to 4½ hours, exclusive of stops
Grade	Basic walk is moderate, and the climbs are steady. With the extensions the grade is Hard
Start	Red Lion, Litton. Map reference: 164753
Map	OS Explorer OL24 The Peak District, White Peak Area
How to get there by bus	The village enjoys a daily service from Bakewell, Buxton, Chesterfield and Sheffield, which calls at the bus stop in the heart of the village
How to get there by car	Travel on the A623. Turn off this road at the Anchor Inn near Tideswell or at the turning just west of Wardlow Mires. Both are signposted for Litton. There's a limited amount of on-street parking in the village, but please park with consideration for residents. Alternative parking is available at Tideswell Dale car park, just off the B6049 south of Tideswell and on the route of the walk. The car park is pay and display and there are toilet facilities

The Pub

The Red Lion

The Red Lion at Litton (tel: 01298 871458) is one of the loveliest village pubs remaining in the Peak District. Enter the pub and there are three different rooms, all of which are comfortable for the walker. In winter there are roaring fires and it is difficult to prise yourself away as the light of the day fades. Needless to say, the bus stops are nearby when you eventually gather yourself together. This is a place where comfort and tradition seem to go hand in hand. There are numerous interesting photographs adorning the walls and the combination of stone and woodwork throughout makes it a homely hostelry. Watch out for the sleeping cat in the bar. You'll not disturb it.

The bar is in the far room and a row of hand pulls offer a range of beers including Abbeydale Absolution, Oakwell Barnsley and a couple of guests such as Buxton SPA and Blue Monkey 99 Red Baboons, although these often vary. Walkers are most welcome as are dogs too. Families usually use the room in the rear of the pub but children must be over six years of age. The Red Lion offers a wide selection of food and is not given over to being a gastro pub – it prides itself in maintaining that balance of being essentially a village pub whilst at the same time serving good food for the visitor. There's also accommodation available.

The Red Lion is open from 12 noon until 11pm Monday to Thursdays; to midnight on Fridays and Saturdays and 10.30 pm on Sundays. Food is served from 12 noon until 2pm and between 6pm and 8pm in the evening. Unusually, there's an entire gluten-free menu too. In the summer people spill out onto the village green often to sit and watch the world go by and why not? All in all, this is a delightful village pub, maintaining the balance between catering well for the walker whilst serving the needs of the local community.

The Walk

From the entrance to the Red Lion public house, go left past the school and along the main street. On the right is the old shop and post office, known as The Old Smithy, where refreshment can also be obtained. Go past the road signposted to Cressbrook and Monsal Dale and continue along the main street until you spot a footpath sign on the left hand side of the road, but pointing across the road to an entrance-way between two properties. Turn right here and alongside a step stile, you'll see one of the ubiquitous Peak & Northern Foot Paths Society's green metal signs. Go over the stile and bear left across the field heading for Tansley Dale. The path gives out into a rough walled lane. Turn left here, but almost at once go right, over another step stile and back into fields again. Wardlow Hay Cop is in view ahead and to the right, but as it so nicely says in The Bible, between you and it "there's a great gulf fixed". Bear left to another P&NFPS sign at a wall corner and thus locate a stile. You are about to enter Tansley Dale, part of the Cressbrook Dale National Nature Reserve. Please take especial care in the Reserve, which is famed for its variety of plant life. Spring is the ideal time to visit, but then be prepared to spend a

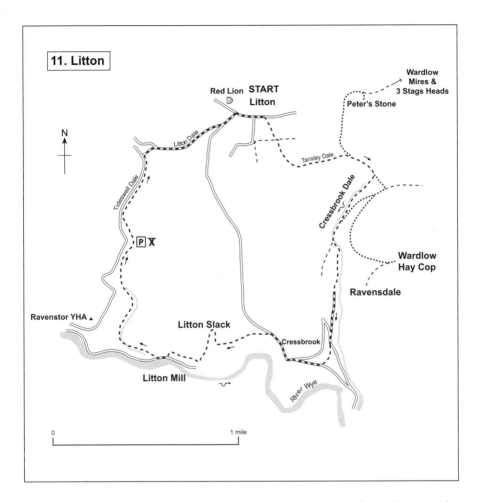

longer time on the walk than outlined in the introduction above. Go over the stile and bear right, descending alongside a derelict wall into the dale bottom. Then follow the obvious path down the dale. The path is quite steep in places and the limestone can be slippery, so please do take care. When the walk was recce'd there was snow on the path and in these conditions it cannot be recommended.

At the bottom of the dale you enter Cressbrook Dale. Go through a small gate and over a set of stepping-stones. More often than not, there's no water to step over, but every now and then you'll be glad of the stones.

Once on the far side of the "stream" it's decision time.

Ascent of Peter's Stone

If you are going to Peter's Stone you need to turn left here and make your way up Cressbrook Dale. Peter's Stone is not in view at this stage, but as you round the bend you'll see it on the right. Indeed you can't miss it. The best ascent is to go round the back and scale it from there. Don't try the full frontal ascent (or descent) unless you have a death wish. Speaking of death wishes, it is worth bearing in mind that the other name for Peter's Stone is Gibbet Rock. In this context it was the scene of the last gibbeting in Derbyshire in 1815. Apparently people came from far and wide to see the grisly spectacle, so much so that a Methodist minister, noting that his congregation was seriously diminished, found them at the site and preached to them in the open air. In this he was following in the footsteps of William Bagshawe, the Apostle of the Peak who is also reputed to have preached to a crowd from the rock in the late 17th century. Interestingly, given the nonconformist religious use of the stone, the name Peter's Stone is said to derive from the similarity of the rock to the dome of St Peter's in Rome! (Some people might be tempted to go even further up the dale to the main road where, on the opposite side of the road, is the Three Stags' Heads, a legendary pub with stone floors and a superb range (the fire) in the bar. The additional distance and time for a visit to the Three Stags is not included in this walk). Having climbed the stone, retrace your steps to the stepping-stones for decision number two.

Ascent of Wardlow Hay Cop

From the stepping-stones, go down the dale for a short distance to the point where the path skirts round the back of a fenced off lead mine entrance. (If you are not going up the Cop, skip to the next paragraph). Those bound for Wardlow Hay Cop keep left here and go up the gently rising path that makes its way up to the crest of the dale. Here it reaches a stile in the upper boundary wall. Bear right as you near the stile and follow a sketchy path beside the wall until you reach a new gate, complete with the Access Land sign. The summit of the Cop can be seen quite clearly and you can make a beeline for it. The view is tremendous from the top and worth the extra effort. Return the same way and when you reach the point where you turned off the public footpath, turn sharp left to descend into the dale again on a different path from that by which you ascended. This path drops down through woodland to rejoin the dale-bottom path, just before the footbridge. (Now skip the next paragraph)

Cressbrook Dale and Ravensdale

From the fenced off mine working, carry on down the dale, noting that you now have a stream accompanying you. This emerged from the mine workings

Cressbrook Dale from Wardlow Hay Cop

and runs more or less all the time. Shortly you enter woodland and the path twists and turns its way through the trees and scrub, sometimes almost in the stream, sometimes well above it. A delightful walk but you need to take care because of the tree roots and the polished limestone. Soon you are joined by a path running down from the left. This is where your more energetic companions rejoin, having been up Wardlow Hay Cop.

Descend to the footbridge and bear left, still following the stream. Ignore the path going off to the right, (unless you've had

Ravensdale

enough and want to get back to Litton more quickly). The dale bottom path continues to twist and turn through woodland until you reach a gate and stile by a water trough. This is the hamlet of Ravensdale. As you pass the cottages look up at the towering limestone crags, a playground for rock climbers.

Cressbrook to Litton Mill

From Ravensdale, follow the tarmacked lane, which rises gently to join the Monsal Head to Litton road. Go straight across the road onto a footpath and continue upwards to join another, narrower road in Cressbrook village. Bear left here, following the road down a short way to a crossroads. The route straight ahead leads only to Cressbrook Hall. Your way is to the right, up the hill. This is the steepest ascent on the entire walk – assuming you haven't attempted either Peter's Stone or Wardlow Hay Cop, but it is easy and soon over. At the top of the hill the road levels out and you have a view down Monsal Dale to Monsal Head. Continuing along the road, with a nature reserve on your left and you soon pass the small church of St. John the Evangelist on the right. Just beyond this, bear left along a rough track, signposted to Litton Mill and Millers Dale.

This track begins as a narrow walled lane, but soon emerges onto open hillside with a superb view down into Water cum Jolly Dale, and a fine vantage point from which to appreciate the precipitous limestone cliffs. You'll also notice a fine stone chimney. The track continues to descend, soon reaching a gate and stile, beyond which is access land. Here you join another track coming down from the right. This is Litton Slack, "slack" being an old word for steep hill. Go left here, soon getting very close to the chimney you saw earlier. This chimney was once part of the Litton Mill complex. These mills gained considerable notoriety in the 19th century because of their harsh employment practices, especially in their use of female and child labour. The exposure of this appalling treatment was instrumental in bringing about the first factory acts, which regulated the employment of children and introduced the idea of an independent factory inspectorate. From the chimney, the track swings sharp right an into a side dale, with a very steep grassy slope on the left. This was the scene of an escapade by one of the authors of this book when he and a colleague decided to take a short cut from Cressbrook to Millers Dale in the author's car. We got as far as this hairpin bend and viewed the remaining descent with alarm. Turning round was not an option (as you'll see), nor was reversing, so down we went. At one point, my colleague decided that he would be better off getting out and making sure that the car didn't go over the edge. A wise move and it is a pity the author couldn't do the same. Incredibly we got down in one piece, but I've never attempted it again, and nor should you.

Stroll down the track, which drops into the side dale and then turns sharp left to reach the cottages of Litton Mill. It would be possible to descend the grassy slope more or less direct, but the track is easier and more comfortable.

Beware giant water "rats"?

A gate and stile takes you into Litton Mill hamlet. The mill complex, which is now private housing, is to the left. Your route is along the road, passing the cottages. The River Wye is to your left and you walk parallel to this for a short distance, until you reach a small car park. Here there's a signpost to Tideswell Dale. Bear right here along a broad track, leaving the main dale behind.

The rest of the walk is little more than a gentle stroll, first up Tideswell Dale, which is delightful. Look out for a cave on the right just before a bridge over the stream. Also look upwards to see Ravenstor Youth Hostel, perched on its craggy outcrop of rock. Thereafter, the valley narrows appreciably before widening out again as you approach another bridge. There are paths both sides of the stream and each path has seats. As both paths go to the same place it is immaterial which you choose, as long as you keep by the stream. Where the two paths converge again the bridge is guarded by a very large water "rat", but it turns out to be harmless. A short distance further on brings you to Tideswell Dale car park and picnic site.

Leave the car park by a footpath close to the vehicular entrance and follow this path, which runs parallel to the road and soon enters access land. The road is just over the wall to your left and there's a roadside footway, albeit on the far side of the road, so the field path is preferable except possibly when it is really muddy. Eventually you reach the end of the access land and the path disgorges onto the roadside, just by the junction for Litton. Turn right here into Litton Dale and follow the road, which again has a footway. Where the footway ends, on the outskirts of the village, it is possible to avoid further road walking by using a series of field paths to the right, but this is not recommended. Instead, continue along the road into the village centre, there locating The Red Lion and the end of this walk.

Walk 12. Longnor to Hartington

The Route	Longnor, Beggar's Bridge, Crowdecote, Pilsbury Castle, (optional ascent of Carder Low), Hartington
Distance	5.6 miles (9 km). 625 feet of ascent (192 metres). Allow 3 hours exclusive of stops. The optional ascent of Carder Low adds a further ½ mile (0.8km), 225 feet of ascent (70 metres) and a good 20 minutes to the walk
Grade	Moderate point-to-point walk with some unforgettable climbs
Start	Longnor Market Square. Map reference: 088648
Map	OS Explorer OL24 The Peak District, White Peak Area
How to get there by bus	There's a daily service, High Peak 442, from Ashbourne and Buxton, which forms the main public transport artery in this part of the Peak District. The bus picks up in the Market Place in Hartington as well as in Longnor. The demand responsive service, Moorlands Connect serves Longnor on Mondays to Saturdays, telephone 0300 1118003 for details
How to get there by car	As this is a linear walk you'll have to use the bus at some stage. For Longnor, travel on the B5053 from Brierlow Bar near Buxton or from Bottom House near Leek. There's car parking in the Square and at other village car parks. Avoid busy summer Sundays. Hartington is signed off the A515 (Buxton-Ashbourne) road and from the B5053 just north of Warslow. The authors always prefer to do the bus journey first, in order to avoid having to rush a walk to catch a bus at the end. In this case, it would be best to park at Hartington and catch the bus to Longnor (Market Square) – it is about a 20-minute journey. However, note that Hartington get extremely busy at weekends and on-street parking will be at a premium.

The Pubs

The Packhorse

The Packhorse at Crowdecote (tel: 01298 83618) is aptly named for in years gone by it would have served many a weary 'jaeger' or 'jagger', the men who looked after trains of packhorses on their journey through the Peak District. The pub has two separate areas around a central bar with lots of comfortable places to take a rest; walkers are welcome whatever the season.

The Packhorse usually stocks three to four cask ales including at least two local brews in the CAMRA local promotion. The usual opening times are from 12 noon until 3pm and from 6pm in the evening. Food (home-cooked) is served from 12 noon until 2.30pm and from 6pm to 9pm. The bad news is that the Packhorse is not open on Mondays and Tuesdays so don't do the walk early in the week! Families are welcome and there are seats outside and a beautiful south facing garden for those warmer days.

Hartington pubs

On arrival at Hartington, there are two old coaching inns around the market square; the Charles Cotton Hotel and the Devonshire Arms both of which offers several real ales, although you are more likely to find local stuff at the Charles Cotton. There's also Hartington Youth Hostel at Hartington Hall, about 5 minutes walk from the centre on the Biggin Road. It has a bar serving local real ales and has built a deservedly good reputation for food.

The Walk

Longnor

The bus arrives in Longnor Market Square and there's a feeling you are stepping back in time; the pace seems slow and not much has changed recent decades other than the loss of shops and pubs. Some say that Longnor is a place for longevity for, in the churchyard behind the Market Square, lies the grave of one-time resident William Billinge. He lived in the 17th and 18th centuries, reaching the ripe old age of 112. What is surprising is his epitaph which cites his career in the army and the battles he participated in at home and abroad. The words on his gravestone read:

> *Billeted by death*
> *I quartered here remain*
> *When the trumpet sounds*
> *I'll rise and March again.*

Longnor has long been a favourite gathering place for walkers and but the pub scene has declined in recent years as one has closed and the other no longer trades as a public hotel and bar. But there's the café and craft centre. Longnor's old market hall dates from 1873 and still has a list of tolls. There are many similar features around this shy little town, which provide insights into its importance in North Staffordshire in earlier years. Evidently, the only major irritation for the populace is parking and you can see why when a group of ramblers meet here for a circular walk. That is why we suggest that you catch bus the bus up from Hartington and walk back!

From the Crewe and Harpur Arms in Longnor, a fine building in its own right, turn right to walk up the main street, passing the cosy looking Cheshire Cheese public house (a Robinson's house) on the left. Continue to climb and just beyond the last cottage (known as Town End), turn left and walk up the road, which bends left to a point called Top o' th' Edge (signed as such). What a view from here across the pastures of the upper Dove and to the unusual shapes of Aldery, Hitter, Parkhouse and Chrome hills – the dramatic reef limestone formations which characterise the upper reaches of Dovedale.

Parkhouse and Chrome Hills from Glutton

Beggar's Bridge

At the fork in the road, keep right and go through the metal barred gate to drop down the hillside. It descends to a gate and then to a barn where you leave the track, which is all to the good as it leads to a small sewage works.

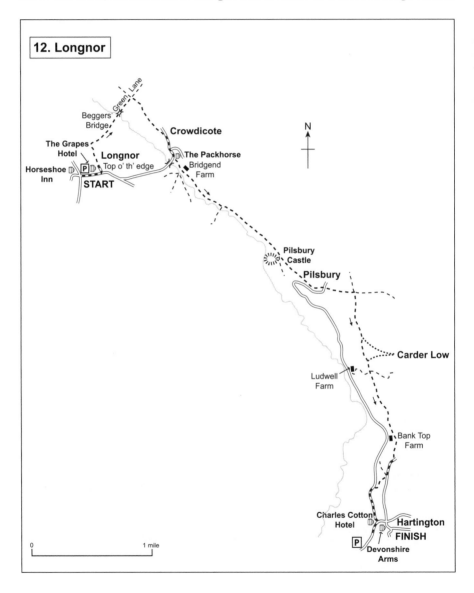

The path runs along the left-hand side of the barn and then cuts right as indicated by the finger post. There before you is a well-worn path running ahead through wet ground. It rises over gentle folds in the field to a small rise before dipping down, slightly left, to Beggar's Bridge spanning the River Dove. Such names are always intriguing and one wonders how many thieves have lain in wait for packhorses at this lonely spot. Longnor was certainly a key market place in previous centuries attracting trade from nearby villages and farmsteads; there would have many a journey to market along these very paths providing fine pickings for the 17th-century footpad.

Crowdecote

Step across the bridge to Derbyshire, imperceptible perhaps, but for much of its course the Dove is a political boundary. The path becomes a really wide strip, bounded by neat drystone walls, evidence that this was once a major thoroughfare. You will note a barn across to the left and a gate ahead and at this point there's also one on the right. Go over the stile to the right of a large gate and then immediately right over a step stile. Continue ahead with a fence and wall to the left over a step stile until you reach a barred gate, which leads to a track. Follow this all of the way into the hamlet of Crowdecote, not much changed over the decades, where you reach a road. Turn right and right again to follow the road around to the Packhorse pub.

If not imbibing, go ahead to pass two snug cottages sitting by the road. Where the road swings away to the right, you go ahead on a track towards Bridge End Farm. Keep to the lower (right) track but do not go right towards the footbridge when you reach the gate. Your way is ahead through the yard and by a barn. The path is waymarked. Once through a gate keep ahead on the track. This follows a line almost parallel with the meandering River Dove and you cross another step-stile next to a gate.

Pilsbury Castle

The tractor track gives out into a large field and peters out into a path, which is well-trodden. Keep ahead mid-field and cross a stile, track and gate before approaching Pilsbury Castle Hills. The castle mounds, so distinctive on the landscape, challenge the inquisitive mind. Why here? What would it have been defending? Pilsbury is no more than a few dwellings in the middle of nowhere.

Cross a kissing gate and stile and here are the answers to your questions about the castle. There's an interpretation board on your right explaining the nature of the site you are about to pass through. It is clearly a strong defensive site and there's a major river crossing nearby. There were also territorial lands to protect. In all, this was clearly an important site and the remains have been described as one of Derbyshire's finest surviving motte and bailey mounds. Pilsbury Castle, however, was not built of stone like Peveril Castle at Castleton. It was an earlier prototype, a wooden palisade structure with a tower and few accompanying buildings. In this particular case, there was no lord sufficiently interested to rebuild this fortress in stone. Building a castle was an expensive capital outlay, akin to major regeneration schemes today and a twenty-five year project to boot. According to the historians there's no firm evidence to support the argument that it was in use as a fortification beyond the 14th century.

The path rises sharply up the hillside to the left of the main mounds so take another breath and gird yourself for the climb out of the valley, ignoring the first gate on the left. Go through a gateway and continue to rise up the hillside, ignoring the path on the right descending into the valley. You climb up to a step stile at the brow. Cross this and keep company with the drystone wall on the left. Climb the next stone step stile and go ahead for 20 yards/metres or so. Now go through a small gate and head slightly left in this field aiming for a point to the right of the buildings. It seems strange to exit onto a road, a gated and lonely thoroughfare running between Hartington and Sparklow.

Carder Low

Cross over the road and a stile. The path runs ahead to pass through a break in a drystone wall, where there's a large upright stone as a marker. Continue ahead to pass another large stone. Keep ahead until you approach the next wall but at this point bear right to climb up the bank.

Cross a step stile, go ahead at first, then head slightly left as way-marked at the field boundary corner. The same applies at the next field corner as you make your way along the lower edges of Carder Low. The place name "Low" is a corruption of the Norse "hlaw", meaning "hill". It is a common place-name in Derbyshire and causes some consternation by seeming to mean the exact opposite. Carder Low was an ancient burial site and has also been the subject of surface mining in the past. The hill is now access land and the (380 metre) summit can easily be gained from the path. The view from the top is worth the climb, but make sure you've sufficient time if you have a bus to catch in Hartington. The path descends the hillside but make sure that you keep more or less ahead beneath the outcrop and by trees.

Cross a small gate at the barred gate and continue ahead to squeeze through a gap stile in the next boundary. It is about 30 yards/metres to the right of the gate. In the next field head slightly right and pass through a small spring-loaded gate. Now head slightly left to rise up again and then proceed ahead.

The path dips to cross a stile in the next wall and, once over, keep ahead again to cross another stile. In the next field, head very slightly right. Go through a gateway and it is ahead once more. The path descends between strewn limestone rocks, which have been previously worked, and passes by the remnants of a wall. Keep your height here as you walk between hawthorns. Another path joins by the corner of the wall and you continue forward with the drystone wall to the left.

The path comes to a barred gate and concrete road. Go left to climb up. There's a bird's-eye view of Bank Top Farm below. To the right of the barred gate is a small gate leading into the field. Once through go immediately right to keep company with the wall on the right. In about 100-150 yards/metres, there's a step stile to cross. Once over, maintain a path ahead. Go over a stile and head slightly left across the field. Rise up once more to cross another step stile and aim for the right of the barn.

Exit onto the road and turn right. Just before the building on the left there's a green lane off to the right. Descend this to join another lane near to Moat Hall. Turn left to walk into Hartington, which after all of that open space and the reel of dramatic views (unless you were unlucky enough to be walking in a shroud of mist) seems crowded with people. The delights of Hartington await you; the duck pond, village green, cheese shop, farmers' market and a couple of pubs. If catching the bus, the stop is centrally located in the market place.

Walk 13. Matlock

The Route	Matlock railway station, Masson Farm, Heights of Abraham, Ember Lane, Bonsall, Pounder Lane, Masson Lees
Distance	4¼ miles (7 km). 1157 feet of ascent (353 metres). Allow at least 2½ hours exclusive of stops
Grade	Moderate but with several sharp climbs
Start	Matlock railway station. Map reference: 296602
Map	OS Explorer OL24 The Peak District, White Peak Area
How to get there by bus	Daily buses from Alfreton, Ashbourne, Bakewell, Buxton, Chesterfield, Sheffield, Derby, Nottingham, Manchester and Stockport call at one or other of the two bus stations, one of which is located adjacent to the Co-op supermarket, the other next to the railway station
How to get there by car	A6 from Derby or Buxton directions. A632 from Chesterfield. A617 from Alfreton. There's long-stay parking adjacent to the railway station, but it is pay and display
How to get there by train	Daily trains from Derby and Nottingham

The Pubs

We are featuring two pubs in Bonsall for they are both exceptional survivors from a much larger range of hostelries located in the village in earlier decades.

King's Head

The first is The King's Head, (tel: 01629 822703), a two-roomed local offering a warm welcome to ramblers. In winter, the seat near to the stove is a very popular option. The King depicted on the inn sign is Charles II, which equates with the date of the pub opening, 1677, though local word says that it was opened on the day King Charles I was executed in January 1649. Either way it's a strange choice of name, given that the area was well known for its support of Parliament during the Civil War. The first landlord engraved his name on one of the beams when his first son was born here.

The King's Head is open at lunchtimes on Saturdays and Sundays only, except Bank Holidays. It is open in the evenings at 21.00 on Monday and from 18.30 Tuesday to Saturday (19.00 on Sundays). Food is served Tuesdays to Sundays and on Bank Holiday Mondays. It welcomes families and has a patio area outside. The real ales are Bateman's XB, plus two guest beers. Parties of 10 or over wishing to avail themselves of refreshment on weekday lunchtimes are asked to contact the landlord and wherever practical, the pub will be opened for them.

Barley Mow

The other pub is The Barley Mow (tel: 01629 825685) a short detour from the route of the walk through Bonsall, but worth the extra distance. This welcoming pub hosts a wide range of events, including: the annual World Championship hen race held in August and the landlord's guided walks on Bank Holiday Mondays and after Christmas. Take a look at the pub website for updates: www.barleymowbonsall.co.uk. As the website suggests, the pub is; "Famous for hosting the 'World Championship Hen Races', (1st Saturday in August) and also for being officially the most likely place to be abducted by Aliens in Europe. The Barley Mow is an exciting yet sometimes strange place...." The pub was awarded CAMRA 'Pub of the Year' for Matlock and Dales area 2011. This is a traditional pub with beams and brasses and a stone fireplace where people gather around. It is also a lively pub, which thrives on community spirit and encourages local people to join in and hold their society meetings here. There's always a good range of real ales on offer; an ever changing selection of fine ales from all over the country, as well as locally produced beers. The pub is accredited with the CAMRA Locale scheme (20 miles or less from the pub). The Barley Mow is open from 6pm to 11pm Tuesday to Friday evenings, and all day from 12 noon at weekends. Food is served from 6pm to 9pm on Tuesday to Fridays and 12 noon to 3pm and 6pm to 9pm on weekends and Bank Holidays. Please note the pub is usually closed Mondays, except Bank Holidays. Families are welcome. Yes, make that detour.

The Walk

Matlock to Heights of Abraham

Walk down the station approach, avoiding the bridge supports! At the junction of the A6 and Snitterton Road, at the traffic lights by the Royal Bank of Scotland, go right. Walk up Snitterton Road for a short distance and then bear left where a signpost indicates the Limestone Way. Go up past the houses, up the steps and into a steep field. Climb the field until you reach a waymarker

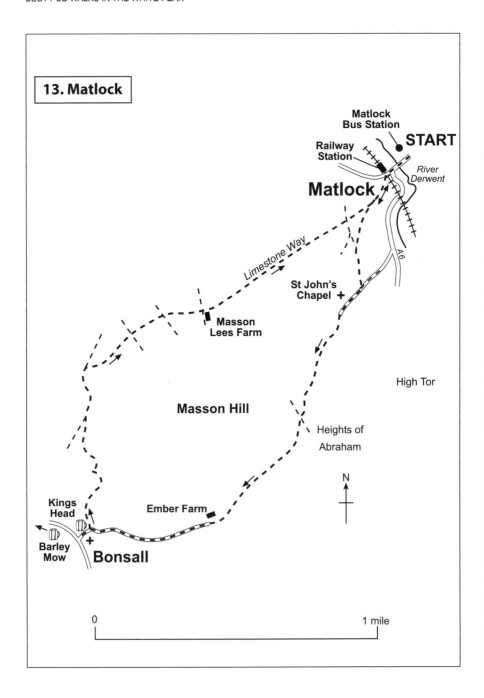

13. Matlock

and here bear left, soon passing through a stile. Cross the next field, passing through a gap in the wall. There are good views from here over to Riber and right across Matlock. Cross the next field and then a stile leads onto a rough track. This dips in and out of a small dale, round the back of a former quarry, before reaching St John's Road. Walk up the road, passing the chapel on your right and noting the massive water troughs built into the wall. The chapel is now in the care of the "Friends of Friendless Churches", and is of considerable architectural interest, especially for people keen on Victorian building and décor. Services are still held here on occasions and are an interesting experience as there's no electric light.

At the end of the lane, bear right, following a path signed to the Heights of Abraham. This path passes over some smooth and slippery limestone that rarely seems to dry out completely, so take care. The path passes through an area of scrub and round the back of a farm before reaching open fields, where there's a view ahead to the Victoria Tower on the Heights of Abraham. Bear right, following the waymarked path across the field and through a stile onto Masson hillside. The path twists and turns through scrub, steadily rising until you reach the tarmacked path from the Heights of Abraham to the Masson Mine exit. Cross this track and continue up the hill to a stile/gate on the left, which again is waymarked. The path now drops almost into the Heights of Abraham site before swinging right and following an almost level course through the dense woodland, high above Matlock Bath.

Heights of Abraham to the King's Head

The various hummocks and hollows in the wood and the curious metal grills that you see from time to time, remind you that this was a heavily mined area for lead and fluorspar.

The path eventually emerges from the woodland, fights its way through an area of scrub, then dips and crosses another lead rake. This was last worked in the 1950s for fluorspar. A little further on, at a junction of paths, (virtually a crossroads), go right and enter Ember Lane, near Ember Farm. The lane soon becomes a walled track

Bonsall church

105

with views to the south over the Via Gellia to Black Rocks and Middleton. Follow the lane as it descends gently into Bonsall. Turn right at the T-junction by the church and continue down until you reach the cross in the centre of the village. The King's Head pub is just on your left. If you are bound for the Barley Mow, go down Yeoman Street and then turn right, up The Dale to reach the pub.

Climbing again

On leaving the King's Head, go up to the cross. This is a fine example of a mediaeval market stepped cross. It is reputedly the tallest in Derbyshire.

Go up the narrow lane by the seating area and immediately begin to climb. This lane is one of the many ancient packhorse routes that converge on Bonsall. All were used for the carriage of lead ore from the mines to the smelters. The first section of the lane has a concrete surface as it was used in the 1950s by lorries for transporting the local fluorspar.

Climb steeply away from Bonsall, with increasingly good views over the village to the small hamlets of Uppertown and Slayley. A network of narrow lanes and paths links these settlements more directly than the motorable roads. Some of these pedestrian routes can be seen as walled lanes as you look across the valley.

The concrete surface finishes at a gateway where the track to the mines continued up the hillside, where there are obvious traces of mineral working. This was part of the Great Rake, which outcrops extensively on the eastern side of the hill at Matlock Bath. You crossed it earlier on the approach to the Heights of Abraham. Your way now goes left, levels out and narrows appreciably, though still running between stone walls. It can be decidedly muddy at times. A short distance further on, there's a chance to break out of the confines of the lane where a footpath joins from the left. From this point on, there are two rights of way, the lane itself and, beside it, on the left in the field, a footpath. Those wishing to avoid mud should use the latter route, which parallels the lane. This dual rights of way situation is not uncommon in Derbyshire. The reasoning behind it was that pedestrians could walk away from the heavily used packhorse route, thereby avoiding both the horses and the resultant mud and muck. To a large extent this is still a valid justification, for the lane is still used by horses and also cyclists, both pedal and motor.

Leadwort and Alpine Pennycress

Continue along the lane or the adjacent path, with fine views of Bonsall and Via Gellia to your left and the remains of fluorspar workings to your right. These are now almost completely revegetated and rapidly developing into woodland. Really old workings are readily identified by the line of hummocks and hollows, basically spoil heaps and shafts. These are characterised by a distinctive lead tolerant flora such as the delicate white flowers of Minuatiae Verna, known locally as Leadwort, or the equally delicate Thlaspi Alpestri, or Alpine Pennycress. Newer workings tend to suffer from the modern disease of "instant restoration" with the hummocks being flattened, opencast pits back-filled and the new surface given a liberal dose of "motorway mixture" to secure quick grass growth. Unfortunately the lead tolerant species lose out by this process and surveys of the "modern" workings on your right have revealed neither Leadwort nor Alpine Pennycress.

Pounder Lane to Masson

If you've been using the path rather than the lane, the two rejoin for a final muddy slide down the junction with another deep-cut hollow-way. This is Pounder Lane. Turn right and resume the ascent. The hollow-way soon widens out, being the access point for the 1950s workings. The parallel footpath also resumes; again on the left-hand side, but this time there's little or no boundary between the two, the wall or hedge having been largely removed to widen the lane for lorries. The path rejoins the lane at a gateway, but this is not too obvious. The view back from here extends to Harboro' Rocks and Golconda Mine (now Viaton Industries, but still engaged in mineral processing). Where the path rejoins, there's a veritable conglomeration of routes. A path carries on northwards over a stile. This is a continuation of the packhorse route, heading now for Jug Holes and Darley Dale. Pounder Lane continues ahead, through a gate, making for Salters Lane and Matlock. Your way is a third route, no more than a path, but signed, passing through a gap stile in the wall on the right and heading east, slightly left across the field between two barns. During the recce for this walk, we were forced to take shelter in the left-hand barn as it had come on to rain.

Go up the field, with the wall to your right. Until recently this field path was bounded either side by stone walls forming a broad green lane. The left-hand wall has now disappeared. This path was part of an ancient route from the Mettesforde over the Derwent (near where Matlock Bridge now stands) to Uppertown and Grangemill, Minninglow and on to Leek. It formed part of the old salt route from Cheshire from which the nearby Salters Lane takes its name.

The path soon emerges onto the broad track once used to access the Masson fluorspar workings. There's a tremendous view over Matlock from here and an equally fine view up the Derwent valley to Rowsley and beyond. Go across the track and over a stile. Bear right, across a corner of the field to another stile, then follow the distinct waymarked path to the left, heading downwards into the Derwent valley. Signs here proclaim that you are on the Limestone Way. You are also in the Masson Site of Special Scientific Interest. The basis of the SSSI designation is the area's immense geological interest, but there's also an abundance of the lead tolerant flora in and around the archaeological remains of lead and fluorspar mining. Legend has it that the Romans worked this hillside for lead and there's certainly evidence of very early mining. In fact the mining remains on Masson cover a period from near Roman times almost to the present day as opencast mining only ceased here in the 1980s.

Beware volcanoes

The geological interest is centred on the fact that Masson Hill comprises a mass of limestone trapped between two layers of volcanic lava. At the junctions of the lava and the limestone there has been a chemical reaction to form Dolomite limestone. In water-formed caverns in the limestone there were rich mineral deposits of galena (lead ore), fluorspar and barytes. Unusually for Derbyshire, the mineralisation did not form very long narrow veins or rakes, but took the form known as "pipes"; hence the pockmarked appearance of Masson hillside. These are the remains of innumerable shafts. Be warned, these relics are very dangerous, though most are now "capped". Do not wander. Keep to the recognised footpaths.

Go down the steepening hillside, soon reaching a track that cuts across the path. This was another access route to the mines. Here you will find Geoff's seat and this is a good place for a rest and a contemplation of the view. From the seat go right for a short distance then left, following the Limestone Way signs. Down the fields you go, to a gate/stile just to the left of Masson Lees Farm. Cross the farm track, go over another gate/stile and then on down the field. The path carries on more or less on this alignment, so ignore any tracks and paths that cross it. Sometimes the hedge is on the left, more often on the right. Sometimes the gates/stiles are hidden in a thicket but they are always there and accessible, because this is the well-walked Limestone Way. After a little over ½ mile of steady descent (about a kilometre), you emerge onto a rough lane and ahead of you is the final plunge into Matlock. Go over the stile and into the field and follow the steep path down until you reach Snitterton Road. You shouldn't need any help now to reach the railway station.

Walk 14. Matlock Bath

The Route	Matlock Bath, Starkholmes, Riber, Hearthstone, Bilberry Knoll, Coombs Wood, Castletop, Wood End, Cromford, Matlock Bath
Distance	5.6 miles (8.9 km). 1233 feet (376 metres) of ascent. Allow 2½ to 3 hours exclusive of stops
Grade	Moderate to hard, with a number of climbs – some fairly steep in places
Start	Matlock Bath railway station (and car park). Map reference: 297585
Map	OS Explorer OL24 The Peak District, White Peak Area
How to get there by bus	Daily buses from Alfreton, Ashbourne, Buxton, Derby, Matlock (of course), Manchester, Stockport and Sheffield
How to get there by car	Daily buses from Alfreton, Ashbourne, Buxton, Derby, Matlock (of course), Manchester, Stockport and Sheffield
How to get there by train	Daily trains from Derby, Nottingham and Matlock to Matlock Bath Station

The Pubs

Princess Victoria

The Princess Victoria (tel: 01629 593458) is situated on the main road (South Parade) in Matlock Bath. It is widely known by its initials, The PV. It has a main bar and an upstairs restaurant. From many spots in the pub it is possible to look out onto the passing crowds of visitors who promenade through Matlock Bath especially at a weekend. Having been closed for some time, the pub is now owned by Ashover Brewery, the same people who run the Old Poets Corner in Ashover. It is therefore not surprising that it prides itself on offering excellent home-made food with friendly service and always having a wide range of cask ales available. Usually there are up to six hand pumps on the go, with regular beers being Bateman's XXXB, Ashover Brewery's Light Rale and Poets Tipple plus other guest beers from various local and not so local small brewers. (Titanic Steerage was on offer when we recce'd the pub). Belgian beers are also available and several traditional ciders.

The pub website describes it thus: "A Real Ale pub in the heart of the village of Matlock Bath, At least 6 Real Ales, Traditional Ciders, Real Fire and Real Character. Well behaved dogs and children are allowed".

The website firmly states that there will not be any Keg or Nitro/smooth bitters, nor TVs, pool tables, games machines or Juke boxes; that's our kind of pub.

The pub is open from 10.00 – 23.00 every day. Food is served. Families are welcome.

Other pubs en route

Matlock Bath is not short of pubs. To reach the PV you will already have passed The Fishpond and closer to the station are The County and Station and The Midland. Near the start of the walk you'll also have passed The White Lion at Starkholmes.

The Walk

Swiss Influence

Matlock Bath station is a grand survival. It was built in the "Swiss cottage" style as befitted a place that even in the 19th century was a major tourist destination, trading on its scenic grandeur. Despite being closed along with other local stations in the 1960s the buildings and platforms were left intact and when common sense prevailed a little later on, restoration and reopening was relatively easy.

The walk begins with a level crossing, which takes the footpath across the railway and is signed to the Heights of Abraham cable cars. Follow the path to the cable car station and consider your options; either a decadent trip to the Heights of Abraham or a pleasant stroll? No contest. Turn right at the cable cars and begin the ascent to Starkholmes and Riber. This path is tarred throughout and rises steadily alongside the High Tor Pleasure Grounds. Ignore the rougher path going off to the right and continue along the tarred path, still climbing. You soon reach the outermost houses of Starkholmes and emerge onto a cul-de-sac. Go right here, up to the main road and then right again. There's a footway on one side of the road.

Up to Riber

When you reach the junction with Riber Road, bear left. Riber Road is steep and now you begin to regret your decision to choose a stroll rather than the cable cars. Looking across the valley you can see the Victoria Tower on the Heights of Abraham and the cable cars ascending and descending easily. The first part of Riber Road is so steep that the footway has steps in it, but thereafter there's no footway at all.

Follow the road uphill to the point where it makes a right-hand hairpin bend and here go straight ahead along a narrow lane by the side of a house called Falconcliffe. Where the lane reaches Falconcliffe House, (not the same place as mentioned earlier), it ends, and a path continues just to the left of the house, looking for all the world like the entrance to their back garden. Nonetheless, it is a public path and you soon leave the house behind and enter fields. This section is actually level. Look out for a spring and trough on the right, probably the local water supply until the mains water was laid on. You pass the replacement facility, Severn Trent's Wards End pumping station on the right. Who was Ward and why did he end it here we wonders?

The path continues distinctly and more or less level through a series of fields, with widening views to the left over Matlock and the Derwent valley. Soon you reach a crossing of paths and here you go right, resuming the ascent to Riber. The castle can be seen on the hilltop and the path is paved, a sure sign of former heavy use. Ignoring the tempting seat, keep climbing, soon crossing a farm drive. Continue upwards, eventually passing through a stile and into a narrow ginnel with Riber Castle on the right. You soon emerge from the confines of the path onto what was the main entrance to the castle.

Riber Castle

Riber Castle has had a chequered history. It is a Victorian construction, built in the 1860s as the home of John Smedley, who made his fortune out of the Matlock hydros. As a house it was not a success, nor was it satisfactory in its later guise as a school. The building fell into ruin and was taken over as a zoo and wildlife sanctuary, specialising in European animals. This venture also foundered eventually and there have since been various schemes to develop the site. At the time of writing (January 2012) the castle is being redeveloped as apartments, along with the construction of some new houses in the extensive grounds. The proposal engendered a lot of local opposition.

Follow the access road down past the squat little tower, noting with some amusement the plastic Expelair in what appears to be a mediaeval battlemented wall. At the junction at the bottom of the drive, go right, but note the superb Jacobean mansion on your left. Riber is blessed with some very fine old buildings, against which the castle is a poor sham. Next along the road is Riber Farm, also Jacobean and this is followed by Riber Hall.

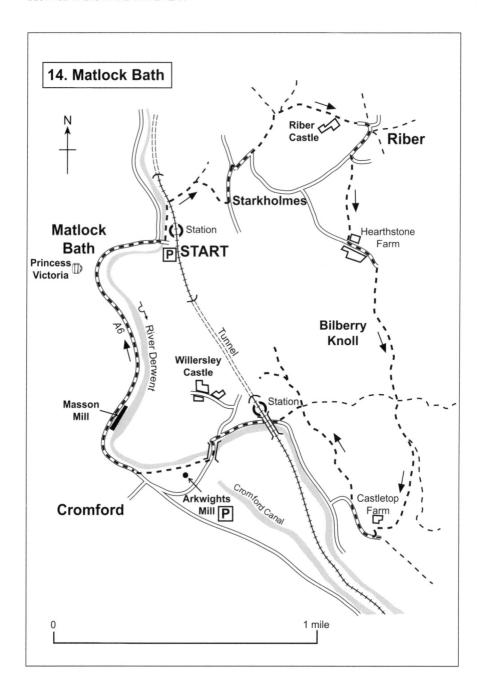

14. Matlock Bath

N

Riber Castle

Riber

Starkholmes

Matlock Bath

Princess Victoria

Station

P START

A6

River Derwent

Tunnel

Hearthstone Farm

Bilberry Knoll

Willersley Castle

Station

Masson Mill

Cromford

Arkwrights Mill P

Cromford Canal

Castletop Farm

0   1 mile

Hearthstone Farm and Bilberry Knoll

At the triangle of roads, go left and then almost immediately right, through a squeezer stile by a telephone pole. The path is signed. Crich Stand, Derbyshire's only lighthouse, can be seen to the left, perched on top of its limestone knoll. Head across the field towards Hearthstone Farm. The first objective is to cross a stile just to the right of a large oak tree. Beyond this point, keep the wall, fence or hedge to your right and cross a number of fields. Soon you reach a stile that leads into new(ish) plantations, where the path is confined between wire fences. In this manner you reach the lane by Hearthstone Farm.

Turn left and pass through the hamlet of Hearthstone, noting the amusing sign warning of children playing. Carry on along the lane, until it forks, by an oak tree. Here go right. The lane, hitherto a tarred road now becomes a fine "green " lane, bounded by gritstone walls.

The lane ascends gently, soon passing a plantation on the left, the western extremity of Littlemoor Wood. To the right is Bilberry Knoll, at 910 feet (280 metres), the highest point reached on this walk. Unfortunately Bilberry Knoll is not accessible and hides the view over the valley, but this is soon remedied. ·

Downhill all the way?

From this point it is (almost) downhill all the way. As the lane begins to descend there's a fine open aspect to the east, south and west. Stroll down the lane enjoying the views and ignoring any paths to right or left.

You soon reach a gate leading into open fields, but the route is still obvious, running as a terrace and with excellent views across the Derwent valley towards Cromford. The house on the knoll to the right is Castletop Farm, but there's no known evidence of a castle here.

The track leaves the fields to become a walled lane again and soon reaches a T-junction with a farm access where you go left. The lane now describes a hairpin bend to the right just by a footpath sign and private access and becomes a proper, tarred road, though narrow and seeing very little traffic. Follow the lane down a little further until you reach the end of the beech wood. Just past this, beyond the electricity pole, there's a stile on the right and this is your route. It is signed.

Downhill no longer

Head across the field, keeping to the left of another electricity pole. The path is clear underfoot and makes unerringly for a well-hidden stile. This stile gives out onto a tumbled landscape, almost certainly the result of landslips. The narrow path passes in front of a trough and spring and heads towards a telegraph pole, where there was once a field boundary. Follow the hedge and wall towards the wood, which now appears ahead. The wall bends left and is joined by a broad green track, but do not follow this. Instead, go straight ahead to a stile, leading into the wood. When this walk was first checked the authors had a good sighting of a green woodpecker here.

The path is easy to follow through the wood and you soon emerge on the other side, to be faced by twin stiles and a confusing way-mark. Go left here and descend alongside the wood on a narrow path, soon reaching the Holloway-Cromford road. Here go right, soon passing under the railway bridge. If you are worn out by now, you could always go up the steps on the right and catch a train back to Matlock Bath. They run every hour. Otherwise continue along the road. There's a footway.

Of Mills and water power

Cross over the junction with Willersley Lane and carry on, passing the entrance to Willersley Castle.

This was built between 1790 and 1792 as the residence for Sir Richard Arkwright, but he never lived to see its completion. It was the home of Arkwright's descendants until 1922 and is now owned by Christian Guild Holidays. The grounds are extensive and include the land right down to the river. Unfortunately this means that the riverside path is private, unless you are staying at the hotel or are lucky enough to be around on one of the few days of the year that the general public are allowed access. Assuming that neither of these is the case, carry on along the road, soon crossing over the Derwent on the medieval Cromford Bridge. Take care. Although there's a footway it is narrow and so is the road itself so two vehicles have to squeeze past one another. On the far side of the bridge is the fishing temple, a curious little building in sad need of tender loving care. Continuing along the road you come to Cromford church, the canal basin and Arkwright's Mill.

There's much to see here as one might expect from an area designated a World Heritage Site. Buildings from various stages of the mill's development are extant and in particular there's interpretation of the use of water-power, because it was the linking of this with machinery that turned these mills into the catalyst for the 18th century industrial revolution. In 1769, Richard Arkwright patented a water frame for carding and spinning cotton. He chose the site at Cromford because it had year-round water supply. The first mill was five storeys high and from 1772, ran day and night. Initially 200 workers were employed but this rapidly increased to 1000. Arkwright built housing for these workers and examples of this housing can be seen on Cromford Hill. By the time of his death in 1792, Sir Richard Arkwright was reputedly the wealthiest untitled person in Britain. As a cotton mill, operation ceased on this site in the nineteenth century. The buildings were used for various other purposes, eventually ending up as a dye works. By this time many of the buildings were in a decrepit and almost ruinous state and in any case badly polluted, but in 1979, the Arkwright Society bought the site and are now in the process of restoring and interpreting it. The importance of this site as the first successful cotton spinning factory was finally recognised by its inclusion in the Derwent Valley Mills World Heritage Site in 2001. Adjacent to Arkwright's Mill is the terminal basin of the Cromford Canal. Backed by Arkwright and many other landowners, coal owners and industrialists, the canal obtained its Act of Parliament in 1789. There were a number of constructional difficulties, not least being the Butterley tunnel and the Derwent aqueduct, which had to be rebuilt. The canal opened in 1794 having cost more than twice the original estimate – an all too common occurrence during the canal era – and since. Nevertheless, the canal made a reasonable profit for its shareholders until railway competition took much of the traffic. The canal passed into railway ownership in the 1840's and remained there until 1948, by which time it had been formally closed. The canal basin at Cromford remains intact and little altered from its original state. It is well worth a visit. The church at Cromford was originally intended as a private chapel for Willersley Castle, but the death of Sir Richard Arkwright in 1792 altered that. St. Mary's was completed in 1797. After lengthy neglect, extensive renovation work was carried out, and the church was re-dedicated by the Bishop of Derby in April 2002. The Arkwright family are buried in the small graveyard, and Sir Richard Arkwright is buried beneath the chancel. A visit to the church, canal basin and the mill could easily add an hour or more onto your walk, especially as there's a café at both the canal basin and the mill.

A path leads from the back of the main mill car park to the river and then runs alongside the river under towering limestone cliffs to reach the A6. This route was originally a carriage drive and almost the only way into Matlock Bath before the existing A6 route was developed in the early part of the 19th century.

At the A6, turn right and follow the road, soon reaching another mill complex bearing Arkwright's name. This is Masson Mill, now a major shopping outlet. This too has a restaurant and an excellent museum, so again you could easily add another hour to your trip. Masson Mill was built in 1783 and has been regarded as Arkwright's showpiece. It has undergone many alterations since its inception, with extensions being added to the north and west by 1835, the central section, including the Masson Tower being added in 1911 and finally the southern extension in 1928. Despite numerous changes of ownership, cotton spinning continued on this site until 1991, at which time it was reputedly the oldest continually working cotton mill in the world. The Masson Mills complex was subsequently refurbished as a working textile museum, shopping village, licensed restaurant and conference and exhibition centre. Masson Mill was originally powered by a single waterwheel. This soon proved inadequate and in 1801 there were two wheels at work. Steam power was introduced in 1911, hence the mill chimney. In 1928 the water wheels were decommissioned and replaced by turbines. The mill still utilises water-power to generate its own electricity, feeding the surplus into the National Grid.

Continuing along the road you soon look down over the weir on your right. This is the source of the water for the Masson Mill turbines. It is also the site of the greatest fun and games in the annual Boxing Day raft race. The antics of the rafters trying to get their "vessels" down the weir in one piece have to be seen to be believed.

A short distance further on you pass what used to be the local school on your right. Seen from the riverside it is a multi storey building, but at road

Raft Race, Matlock Bath

level it's little more than bungalow height. The New Bath Hotel now lies to your left. By the start of the 18th century Matlock Bath had already found some fame as a spa town. In the 1740's new spa baths were constructed and in 1802 the New Bath Hotel was built, incorporating the spa baths. It has been in continuous operation ever since and is now a 3* hotel. Then, to your right there's a curious little building, which used to be the ticket office for the long closed Cumberland cavern, one of Matlock Bath's show caves. To your left is Matlock Bath's Holy Trinity church, whilst to your right and below are the river gardens and a bridge over the river. From here the east bank is open for public access, but unless you are resisting the temptations of The PV, you will stay on the road. Pass The Pavilion, with its lead mining museum (another hour added on to the walk, especially if you are accompanied by children) and fishpond, complete with fish. Now you really are in the tourist Mecca of Matlock Bath. At weekends this place is unbelievably busy and it would be a brave person who set out to count the number of parked motorcycles arrayed along the promenade.

Cross the road at the pelican crossing near the fishpond and carry on along the road to The PV. On leaving the pub you can either carry on along the road to the end of the station approach, or go over the Jubilee Bridge (Queen Victoria's Golden Jubilee, 1887) and then follow the east bank path to reach the car park by the station. Note that this option involves a bit more climbing and misses out on The County and Station and The Midland.

Walk 15. Middleton by Wirksworth

The Route	Black Rocks, Steeplehouse, Middleton church, Middleton Moor, Hoptonwood quarries, Arm Lees Farm, Middleton Top, Middleton Incline, Rise End, Steeplehouse, Black Rocks
Distance	Main route, 5.2 miles (8.4 km). 795 feet of ascent (245 metres). Allow 2½ to 3 hours without stops, plus ½ hour if you want a train ride at Steeple Grange. 3.25 (5¼ km) 584 feet (178 Metres) for the shorter version. Allow 1½ to 2 hours exclusive of stops
Grade	Moderate with some hills to climb
Start	Black Rocks car park. Map reference: 282550. Bus stops on B5035 or B5036 a short distance away
Map	OS Explorer OL24 The Peak District, White Peak Area
How to get there by bus	Daily buses from Derby, Matlock, Ashbourne and Bakewell (Trent Barton 6.1)
How to get there by car	B5036 from Cromford (A6) turning left at the top of Cromford Hill to Black Rocks car park (signed). B5023 from Duffield (A6) through Wirksworth then B5036 to top of Cromford Hill then signs to Black Rocks. B5035 from Ashbourne to Middleton and top of Cromford Hill, left onto B5036 then signs to Black Rocks
How to get there by train	Daily trains to Cromford station from Derby, Nottingham and Matlock, but this adds 2½ miles (4km) to the walk, and much of it is uphill. Seasonal trains from Duffield to Wirksworth (Ravenstor). Seasonal trains from Steeplehouse to Middleton Recreation Ground

The Pub

Rising Sun

The Rising Sun at Middleton by Wirksworth (tel: 01629 822420) is a whitewashed roadside house standing at a junction of roads. It was at one time a pub-cum-farm. According to the locals, the ghost of a small child haunts one of the bedrooms at the inn. In the 1950s the then landlord lived on the premises not knowing that there was a secret bedroom boarded up. It was only after he left that he became aware of its existence by observing the position of an external window. After some discussion, the new landlord at that time broke through an internal wall and discovered an empty double bedroom; there was no apparent explanation as to why this room had been sealed off. The mystery still remains.

Because of its proximity to the High Peak Trail, the pub is very popular with walkers and cyclists. The pub is open all day, every day and food is served at lunchtime and early evenings. There's also a beer garden. There's normally a choice of beers available; Wadworth's 6X, Marston's Pedigree, Bass and the local Wirksworth Brewery products have featured, as have guest offerings from local microbreweries at Thornbridge, Wincle and Peakstones Rock.

The Walk

Cromford and High Peak Railway

From Black Rocks car park, make your way onto the High Peak Trail and turn right. You are now on what was once the Cromford and High Peak Railway, opened in 1830 and closed in 1967. It was designed using canal technology with long flat stretches interspersed with steep rope worked inclines in place of locks. The line linked the Peak Forest and Cromford Canals. The opening of the Midland Railway's line through the Peak District in the 1860s meant that the CHP lost its raison d'etre as a through route and parts of it closed in 1892. The section from Buxton through to Cromford carried on until the 1960s, kept in business by a plethora of quarries and associated companies.

Black Rocks was once a gritstone quarry, but many lead mines were sunk in this area, piercing the gritstone to reach the ore bearing limestone underneath. It was apparently once possible to get from Cromford to Wirksworth underground, using the various lead mine tunnels. You are not called upon to do this today.

On the flat

Stroll along the trail. As you come out of the woodland, the views over Matlock Gorge to Riber and Willersley are superb. Willersley Castle was built for Richard Arkwright, of Spinning Jenny fame, who had established highly profitable mills at Cromford. The castle is now a Christian holiday centre. The mills are in the care of the Arkwright Society and are in the process of being restored. They now form a key part of the Derwent Valley Mills World Heritage Site and are well worth a visit.

The trail now passes along the dry stone embankment to Steeplehouse, crossing over the Cromford-Wirksworth road. At Steeplehouse you come to the headquarters of the Steeple Grange Light Railway (SGLR). This little railway runs along a branch off the C&HP. The line rejoiced in the name of "Killers Branch" and served Middleton Quarry and Mine. The SGLR runs passenger trains using mine engines and rolling stock. If you are lucky you may be able to save yourself a bit of walking and get a ride up to their Recreation Ground station. Failing that, turn right, through a gate on the signposted concessionary path and cross the railway to reach Old Porter Lane. Here turn left. Go up Old Porter Lane, paralleling the railway line. At the road junction at the top, take a peep over the wall to your left, to see the railway below. Don't lean over too far.

Go over the main road and up the track opposite, still following the railway line. After a few yards there's a stile on the right and a notice, which says that you are entering a nature reserve. Go through the stile and follow the field boundary on your left towards a small brick barn. On your right is a curious fenced enclosure, which serves no obvious purpose, but is to do with the nature reserve status of the land. At the barn, turn left, through a gate, but pause for a moment to look across towards Black Rocks. At this point you are on the limestone, whereas Black Rocks is gritstone. The hummocky ground you can see in front of you is the remains of years of lead mining. Most of the shafts are securely capped, but it is better not to explore too eagerly.

From the barn, follow the path beside the fence with more hummocky ground on your right. At the next stile/gate you reach the access track to Middleton Recreation Ground. This bears away to the left to a bridge, which spans the Steeple Grange Light Railway. Your route goes more or less straight on as a narrow path, heading for a gap in the thorn thicket seen ahead and not for the more obvious gateway. Just before the gap in the thorn thicket another path trails in from the left.

(If you've availed yourself of a train ride from Steeplehouse to Recreation Ground Bridge, go up the steps and follow the path that bears left, away from the access track to the recreation ground. The path heads for a thorn thicket and there joins the main route).

The path wriggles through the thorns to an unnecessarily waymarked stile and a muddy path then descends alongside a wall, with Middleton village in view ahead and the bulk of Middleton Moor rising behind. To the left are the revegetated spoil tips from Middleton Mine.

This Mine was opened as a quarry in 1846 by William Killer (hence the name "Killers branch" for the railway serving the quarry). Apparently he discovered that he had Hoptonwood limestone on his land whilst he was digging out foundations for a workshop. The quarry supplied some of the stone for the Houses of Parliament along with the already established Hoptonwood Stone Company, who were working the same limestone beds on the other side of Middleton Moor. After the First World War, Middleton Quarry supplied large numbers of the gravestones that can be seen at the various British forces' cemeteries in France and Belgium. This production occasioned a Royal visit by HRH The Prince of Wales (later King Edward VIII) in 1928. In 1954 the quarry ceased production because of the increasing cost of removal of overburden, but by then it had been realised that the stone was of exceptional chemical purity and the decision was taken to extract the stone by mining. In this form the mine expanded under Middleton Moor and at closure the tunnels and chambers amounted to 25 miles (40 km). There was only ever one serious roof collapse, in 1975. The result can be seen as a deep depression on top of the moor, (passed by the alternative shorter route of this walk). The quarry and mine were rail served until 1967, at which point the sugar stone from Middleton was the last revenue earning traffic on the Cromford and High Peak Railway. The mine eventually closed in 2005 and the spoil tips and mine compound are now being redeveloped for light industry.

Soon the path enters a narrow walled green lane and in this manner reaches the back of the churchyard. The former Vicarage is to the right and is almost as big as the church itself. Go left, through a gate and up the steps into the churchyard, skirting to the left of the church to emerge on Middleton Main Street. If you've had enough at this point, you could always go left here and merely stroll down the road to the Rising Sun and await your more energetic colleagues.

Now the climbing begins

Cross the road and go up Hillside opposite. The lane climbs quite sharply and soon you are above most of the houses in Middleton, with views across to Black Rocks, Cromford and Riber.

Eventually the lane ends at a gate. On your right, on a knoll there's an odd square of wall. Closer examination reveals that this wall surrounds a shaft, so no further inspection is recommended. A narrow path leaves the lane head, to the left of the gate and climbs steeply and muddily to reach another rough lane.

(This walk has a number of possible "get out" options. You've already had one at Middleton Main Street and here is the second. You can turn left at this

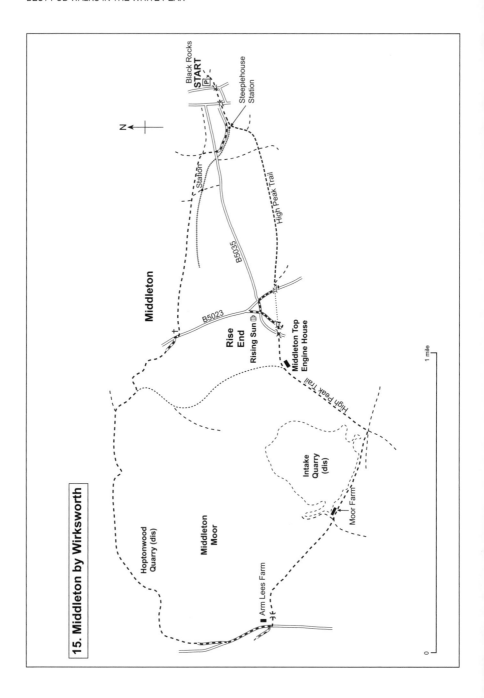

rough lane and by walking a few hundred yards up the lane, passing New Hopton Wood Quarry on your right, to the point opposite the experimental test site, locate a path across the moor direct to Middleton Top engine house, where you will rejoin the main route. This has the distinct advantage of being shorter. You also get an excellent view from the path over the moor and you get to see the site of the 1975 roof collapse in Middleton Mine, which shows on the moor as a huge depression).

The main walk turns right at this point and follows the lane slightly downhill, passing the remains of yet another quarry on the left.

At the T-junction turn left, following a lane marked by a public footpath sign. The road soon deteriorates into a track, which you follow for about ½ mile (800 metres). At this point the track ends at a metal gate, but the footpath branches to the right, going downhill, fenced, walled and rather overgrown, but passable. This lasts for about 100 yards/metres, then the path bears left through a jungle of bracken. Spoil heaps from former lead mining ventures lie all around you and are best left alone. Stick to the path, which despite the bracken, is easy enough to follow. The bracken gives way to scrub and the path begins to descend more steeply, passing a capped shaft to the right and then plunging into woodland as you approach the "back" entrance to Middleton Mine. The path winds its way through revegetated spoil heaps, with good views down into the Via Gellia and then, suddenly, emerges into a picture of desolation and dereliction. This is the former Hopton Quarries, which became part of the Middleton Mine complex. To your left you'll see the securely closed back entrance to Middleton Mine. The link through from the main mine entrance in Middleton village was driven in order to obviate the need for lorries to trundle up and down the village streets and to relocate the crushing plant. It is not, as one of the author's grandchildren described it, the entrance to the Mines of Moria, though it would be a fair representation. The quarry has a long history, beginning in 1789. The Gell family, who owned the quarry, had an access road built to get stone to the Cromford Canal. The resultant road became the Via Gellia, constructed in 1791/2. The quarry was linked to the Cromford and High Peak Railway by a branch line, which opened in the mid 1850's and closed in the mid 1960's Along with Middleton Mine, the quarry closed in 2005, having gone through various ownerships.

Leaving this depressing sight behind, go down the quarry access road. The footpath officially is routed behind a crash barrier, but the route is overgrown and in any case there's no traffic to bother about. When you reach the public road, go left and stroll up the road, under the trees, glad to have escaped Moria unscathed.

After about 250 yards (230 metres) of road walking, you reach Arm Lees Farm. Ignoring the vociferous dogs, turn left at the footpath sign and follow the path through the farm complex to a fine, stone arched bridge. This passes underneath the former railway branch line into Hopton Quarries. Just under the bridge there's a stile on the right. Go through this and bear left following the field boundary. The map clearly shows the right of way as being on the other side of the wall, but in practice this is not the case and attempts to follow it will only lead to problems in the former quarry workings, which can be seen to the left. The path climbs up the field, keeping close to the left hand boundary and soon reaching a stile and gate giving access onto a rough track. Head along the track towards the farm buildings and at the junction of tracks keep straight on, passing the buildings and thus ending up on the High Peak Trail at the point where the access track to Intake Quarry crossed the line. Bear left and follow the High Peak Trail to Middleton Top

Inclined to drink?
Spend some time looking around at Middleton Top and if possible get to see the engine working. The winder, built by the Butterley Company, worked from 1830 to 1963 when it was taken out of use following the closure of the Middleton Incline. This severed the High Peak line into two parts. Note the sections of fish belly rail and the stone block sleepers on the right as you approach the top of the incline and also note the gradient post on the left showing the almost level part of the railway (1 in 1056) and the sudden steepness (1 in 8¼) of the incline. Go down the incline, keeping out of the way of descending cyclists, who are advised to dismount, but usually don't. You soon pass over two bridges. The first is a modern structure, built after the closure of the railway, as part of the Carsington Reservoir project. The second is original C&HP carrying the railway and now the trail over the old main road. Just beyond this bridge there's a sign-posted path to the right, which points to the Rising Sun pub. Go right here, pass under the bridge and follow the old road down to Rise End. The pub is directly opposite.

On leaving the pub, either retrace your steps back up the old road to the bridge and there rejoin the trail, or go down to the cross roads, turn right and follow the main road in the direction of Wirksworth, passing under another bridge and then turning left to rejoin the trail almost at the foot of the incline. Either way, on rejoining the trail, turn right.

Continue down the incline to the bottom, noting the range of buildings below you to the right. This was Middle Peak Wharf, the goods station for Middleton. A branch line continued on from this point to serve Middlepeak quarry. At the foot of the incline there's an information board and the remains

View down Middleton incline

of the wheel pit, complete with wheel. A further information board gives a description of the working arrangements for the wheel.

Continue along the trail, soon reaching yet another information board on the right. This describes the abortive scheme to connect the C&HP line with the Midland Railway's Wirksworth-Duffield branch. The site of the junction can be seen behind the low stone wall. The incline had a gradient of 1 in 4 and the sleeper marks can still be discerned although the tracks were never completed. On the opposite side of the trail is a curious iron structure, which looks like an inverted saddle tank of a locomotive, plus a square iron trough. There has been speculation that this was part of the winding mechanism for the incline to Wirksworth, but if that is the case, it certainly was never completed and operated and it doesn't bear much resemblance to any of the other winding engine sites, though admittedly it would have been of a much later vintage and the designs may have altered.

National Stone Centre and sharks' "teeth"

Still on the Trail, you now come onto another drystone embankment. There's a tremendous view over Wirksworth from here and just below you to the right, is the National Stone Centre's visitor centre. This can be reached by a footpath off the Trail, just beyond the bridge. The Stone Centre examines the history and development of stone quarrying, its methods and how stone is used. The area is fascinating geologically, having been worked continuously for various minerals since at least Saxon times. There are some fine examples of reef limestone, but it is hard to envisage this being a tropical lagoon at one time in pre-history!

Continue along the Trail, noting on your left the overgrown remains of Coalhills hamlet, a former row of quarrymen's houses. There's a long-term restoration plan for these. The Trail now rounds a left-hand bend and Black Rocks comes into view. Just beyond the bend, on the left, is Steeplehouse Quarry, famed for the fossilised "sharks' teeth", found there in great numbers. Steeplehouse Quarry was served by a short branch from the CHPR. A short distance further on, there's yet another information board and you re-encounter Steeplehouse station of the Steeple Grange Light Railway. On the right, the two houses formed the C&HPR's Steeplehouse station and the information board tells the tale of an incident where a locomotive fell off the embankment into the garden.

The walk is nearly over, but you have yet to re-cross the dry stone embankment you traversed earlier and enjoy the view over Cromford and Matlock. Cross the embankment and the Steeple Arch Bridge and so reach Black Rocks again.

WALK 16. MILLER'S DALE

Walk 16. Miller's Dale

The Route	Miller's Dale, Monsal Trail, Chee Dale, Blackwell, Blackwell Hall, Miller's Dale
Distance	5.3 miles (8½ km). 1350 feet of ascent, (415 metres). Allow 3 to 3½ hours exclusive of stops
Grade	Be warned. Whilst this is a beautiful path it is difficult in places (poor surfaces, narrow paths and steep climbs) and can become waterlogged in wet weather. A stick helps. Thus, it is a moderate to difficult walk
Start	Miller's Dale old railway station. Map reference: 138733
Map	OS Explorer OL24 The Peak District, White Peak Area
How to get there by bus	There's a regular daily bus, TM Travel 65/66 serving Miller's Dale from Buxton, Chesterfield and Sheffield. There's also an infrequent Hulley's 68 bus between Buxton and Castleton which calls in the village. The bus stops are near the old railway station
How to get there by car	Travel on the B6049 off the A6 or A623 road to Miller's Dale. Follow the signs to the car park

The Pub

Anglers' Rest

The Angler's Rest (tel: 01298 871323) is an attractive looking pub nestled in the northern bank of Miller's Dale near to the rippling waters of the Wye. The pub is bedecked with ivy and looks very enticing so why not step inside for a while? There are three rooms, a traditional lounge where there's an open fire, a dining room and a rambler's bar that also has a pool area. The pub serves a mixture of locals and walkers as well as visitors passing through the village.

The pub is open from 12 noon until 3pm and from 6.30pm in the evening on Mondays to Fridays. It is open all day from 12 noon on Saturdays and Sundays. Home-made food is served from 12 noon until 2.30pm and from 6.30 – 8.30pm every evening. Hand-pulled beers usually include one from

Adnam's and another from Storm brewery in Macclesfield plus other local beers when there's a rush on. It is in the Good Beer Guide and has won local CAMRA awards so that can't be bad. Families are welcome. Ramblers with boots and dogs are welcome in the Hiker's bar.

The Walk

From the old railway station, walk west in the direction of Topley Pike along the much improved Monsal Trail (improved for cyclists and walkers but can be very busy) The path eases away from the station platforms (refreshments and toilets to be found there on most days) to pass old water tanks and lime kilns said to have opened in the 1890s. Evidently, they were worked until 1944. The kilns can be inspected and interpretation material is provided on site. Not far beyond this point and as you approach the bridge over the River Wye, go right to descend steeply down to the riverside. Turn right and follow the well-worn path alongside the beautiful River Wye. You will soon reach a footbridge to your left over the river. Note this, for although you don't cross it at this stage, it is a landmark on the return route.

Chee Dale

This is where the going gets tougher and you should look carefully at the river. If it is in spate then it would not be wise to continue along the riverside path. Instead you could return to the Monsal Trail and go through the now opened Chee Tor tunnel (though why anyone would want to walk through a tunnel and run the risk of being mown down by cyclists is a mystery). If you do take this option, rejoin the walk at the western end of the tunnel. Continuing along the riverside path you now enter Chee Dale with its swirling pools, narrow gorge, overhanging ledges and richness in plant life, which cannot be matched by many other places.

The Chee Dale nature reserve is part of the Wye Valley Site of Special Scientific Interest. The sheer beauty brings a lump to the throat and stops even the most ardent critics of the national parks in their tracks.

Firstly, you pass through an area of springs and wet flushes as the path eases away from the river to

Chee Tor tunnel, Monsal Trail

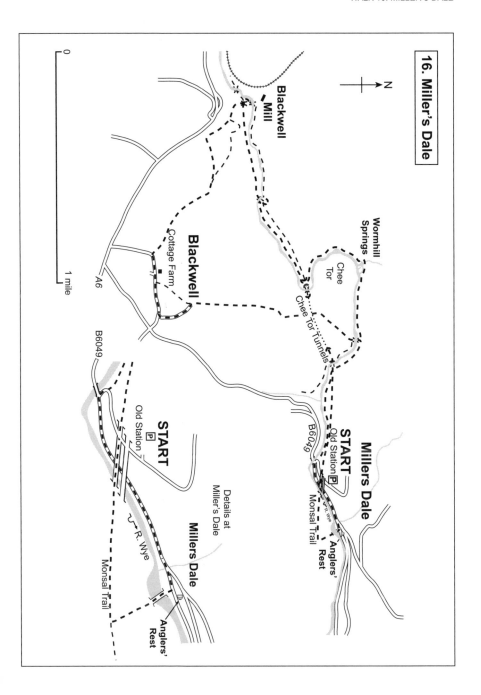

cross a tributary. The water simply bubbles out of the ground and thus encourages a rich biodiversity detailed on an interpretation board. Be sure to stick on the path and avoid any damage to this sensitive environment through which you now pass.

The path returns to the riverside. It is clear enough to follow but requires neat footwork and a fair amount of concentration. It now begins to hug the riverside and that means precise footwork is required as you climb up and down the naturally hewn rocks of the gorge lying beneath Chee Tor. This is a part which is both spectacular and at times wet for there are overhangs with dripping water and the stepping stones along which the path passes are sometimes covered by rushing flood waters. Don't say you weren't warned. The path reaches a footbridge and you cross over and keep ahead upstream under the shadow of the railway track, which is above at this point. The going is easier now and the path leads to a footbridge, which delivers you back to the other side. Keep ahead and you soon reach the next viaduct over the River Wye. However, at a point beneath the arches, go right, pass under the viaduct and climb up to the Monsal Trail. At the top go right and walk along the trail, but not for long. You will see the remains of a railway junction off to the right. This used to be the main line from Derby to Manchester and in the eyes of many it should never have been closed.

You might also note a stile off to the left to Plum Buttress and the nature reserve, but ignore these and continue through the cutting and under the bridge. Now go right to join the Pennine Bridleway (south), which bends to the right to pass over the Monsal Trail by the bridge you came under just a moment ago. Begin to climb on the wide path until you come near to the A6 road. The Pennine Bridleway cuts left and follows a track, for the best part of a mile, (1½ km) through a series of fields to reach a lane near Blackwell village

Blackwell

Go left on the lane into the hamlet of Blackwell. Pass by a caravan park on your left and a farm. Immediately beyond, there's a stile on the left by a wooden gate that is signposted. Go through a small enclosure to the rear of the farm. Cross a stone step stile on the right and walk ahead across the next field. Go through a small gate and head slightly left to go over another stile. Now meander beneath a canopy of trees; note the rich green mosses on the walls. This leads to a step stile and car park, with a large shed to your left.

Keep on a concrete track, with the Farming Life Centre to the left, through a barred gate and onward on a track that runs straight ahead through a gate and between pastures. It begins to descend and eventually curves right to give out into a field. The path then follows the drystone wall on the left down to the dale. As the wall curves left, keep ahead to a small gate. This is not very noticeable until you are almost upon it. Go through this and walk down the steep hillside with a fine view up Chee Dale. The path zig-zags down, passing over the top of Chee Tor tunnel. Your target is the footbridge over the River Wye. Cross over the bridge and go right.

Pass under the masonry viaduct and continue alongside the river, back into Miller's Dale. Go down to the T-junction with the main road and there turn left. Follow the main road with care as there's no footway for some of this stretch. You pass underneath the two great metal viaducts. The first is the original one from the 1860's. The second dates from 1902 when the line was

Monsal Trail at Blackwell Mill

widened. Both are magnificent structures and both are listed buildings. The newer viaduct is in sad need of tender loving care. Where the road forks, bear right to reach the Angler's Rest. Having imbibed sufficiently, locate a footbridge across the Wye and then climb up to the Monsal Trail. Turn right to pass over the older of the two viaducts and thus return to the old station.

An alternative traffic free version of the route described in the preceding paragraph would be to bear left at the masonry viaduct and go up to the Monsal Trail. Retrace your outward route through the station and over the older of the two metal viaducts until you reach a path on the left. This descends steeply to a footbridge over the River Wye and thus reaches the Angler's Rest. To return to the station, retrace your steps over the footbridge, up to and along the Trail.

Walk 17. Monsal Head

The Route	Monsal Head, Monsal viaduct, Brushfield, Litton Mill, Platelayers' path, Cressbrook Mill, Monsal Trail, Monsal viaduct, Monsal Head
Distance	5.3 miles (8.6km). 1454 feet of ascent, (443 metres). Allow 3 to 3½ hours exclusive of stops
Grade	Hard with some steep ascents and descents. Some exposed sections unsuitable for anyone with vertigo
Start	Monsal Head Hotel. Map reference: 185716
Map	OS Explorer OL24 The Peak District, White Peak Area
How to get there by bus	There's a daily bus service, Hulleys 173, from Bakewell, Tideswell and Castleton
How to get there by car	Travel on the B6465 road between the main A623 road at Wardlow Mires and the A6 road at Ashford in The Water

The Pub

Monsal Head Hotel (Stable Bar)
The Stables Bar at the Monsal Head Hotel (tel: 01629 640250) is a firm favourite with walkers and serves a good pint in congenial surroundings. There's a wide range of beers on offer sourced from local micro-breweries, such as Buxton and Hartington, and also a good bar menu. There's also the bar in the hotel itself if the Stables gets very busy. This is an all-day bar. There are tables outside and even in winter-time you'll usually find one or two hardy souls braving it outdoors.

The present Monsal Head Hotel owes its existence to the coming of the railway in the 1860s, when it became the Railway Hotel. However, there was a pub here long before the railway, presumably serving travellers on the Chesterfield to Hernstone Lane Head turnpike. The Stable Bar was originally the stables for the Railway Hotel. Carriages met passengers at Monsal Dale station and conveyed them up the hill to the Hotel. In a sense, with the closure of the railway, the hotel has reverted to its original role, servicing travellers on the roads, which are now infinitely more busy than they ever were in turnpike days.

The Walk

Monsal Dale viaduct

Start from the entrance to the Stables Bar. Turn left along Cressbrook Road and pass a café. The road veers right, plunging into Monsal Dale. There's a view over the viaduct, which is one to be treasured from this vantage point. However, your way is beyond the café, though a gap stile. Turn right, following the signposted route to Upperdale and Monsal Viaduct. This is a very popular path and although you may not have to queue you will be surprised how slowly some people negotiate a perfectly reasonable descent, especially given that there are steps provided. At a junction of paths, turn left, still following the route to the viaduct. This path is much narrower, but still very well used. It descends to a stile, which gives out onto the Monsal Trail just by the western portal of Headstone tunnel. Beware speeding bikes! This tunnel, along with

Monsal Viaduct

others on the Trail was opened to walkers, cyclists and horse riders in 2011. The three main tunnels are lit, but why anyone would want to walk through a tunnel when there's such glorious scenery around defeats me. You'll not go through any tunnels on this walk, unless you particularly want of course.

Cross the viaduct. This was built between 1859 and 1863 as part of the Midland Railway Company's drive to get to Manchester. For just over 100 years it was part of a main line until it succumbed to a round of cuts occasioned by that scourge of the railway network, Dr. Beeching. In fairness it has to be pointed out that Beeching never proposed to close this line. Its closure came about because of machinations elsewhere that are too complicated to go into here. Presumably John Ruskin would now be pleased, bearing in mind his views on this particular route. He saw this viaduct as an eyesore, and castigated the builders in no uncertain terms, "You enterprised a Railroad through the valley - You blasted its rocks away, heaped thousands of tons of shale into its lovely stream. The valley is gone, and the Gods with it; and now every fool in Buxton can be in Bakewell in half an hour, and every

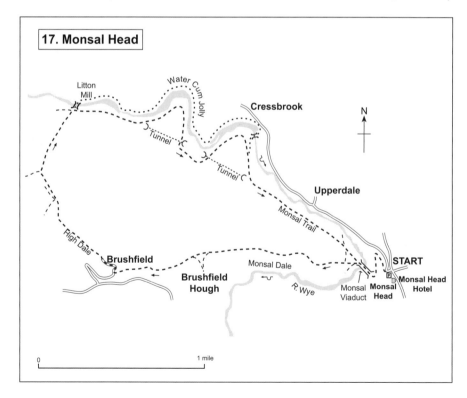

fool in Bakewell at Buxton; which you think a lucrative process of exchange – you Fools everywhere"! Quite what he'd have said to the Lancashire, Derbyshire and East Coast Railway's proposal to build a 300-foot high viaduct across the dale is hard to imagine. This scheme would have seen a viaduct emerging from a tunnel just below the prominent limestone crags on the right hand side of the dale, leaping right across the dale (and the existing railway) to make landfall more or less on the line of the track to Brushfield. Altogether a brave venture, never to be realised, but it would have saved you a considerable descent and re-ascent.

Up to Brushfield

Just beyond the viaduct, leave the Trail to the hordes and go left, following a track signposted to Brushfield. This rises steeply over rough limestone, soon joining another track coming up from the former Monsal Dale station. From here on the track is a public road, though rough, and it is often used by motor-cycles and four wheel drive enthusiasts. At the top of the hill, pause and look back. There's a good view over to Fin Cop, visited on the Great Longstone walk in this book. There's also a good view over to the crags north of Monsal Head. You are standing just about where the high viaduct referred to earlier would have made landfall. From here to Brushfield hamlet you follow the line of the proposed route very closely.

The track progresses easily over the plateau. Initially you'll see various hummocks and hollows just to your left. These are not the abandoned preliminary works for the proposed railway, but are the remains of former lead mines. You'll see better examples later on. Brushfield Hough farm lies to your left and you are soon joined by a track serving this property. Continue straight on. The track is now on a shelf above Taddington Dale and you can hear the rumble of traffic on the A6 far below, but it is hidden in the trees. In this manner you reach the delightful hamlet of Brushfield, now greatly enhanced after what seemed to be years of neglect. Pass through the hamlet, making sure you close the gates and just beyond the last house, go right at the road junction, signposted to Priestcliffe and Millers Dale.

Over to Litton Mill

Climbing away from Brushfield, the lane soon deteriorates to a track which skirts round to the right of Top Farm. There are unusual views from here, up High Dale and to Priestcliffe. The LD&EC railway was intended to run up High Dale and tunnel under Priestcliffe en route to Buxton.

After a steady stroll of about 2/3rd mile (1km) along this grand track, just before a clump of trees, you reach a crossing of paths. Go right, over a signposted stile and follow an ill-defined path beside the wall to a stile by a gate at the far end of the field.

Go over the stile into an area of lead mine remains. These dwarf what you have seen before on this walk. They stretch away to your left and to your right. The view from here is extensive, reaching over to Tideswell and Win Hill; to the Barrel Inn at Bretton and to Wardlow Hay Cop at the top of Scratter. The path turns right and follows the rake across the hillside, then crosses it and begins the steep descent to Litton Mill. A sign proclaims that this is a nature reserve, but it is also open access land. The multiplicity of lead workings should be sufficient to deter all but the most ardent access enthusiast from wandering too far and the advice is to stay on the well-marked path. From here you are looking across Millers Dale to Ravenstor youth hostel and up Tideswell Dale. Continue downhill with the wall close by on your left and with former lead workings everywhere around. Go through a stile by a gate and descend even more steeply with the cottages of Litton Mill now in view ahead. The path wriggles through a patch of scrub to reach a bridge over the Monsal Trail.

Decision time

At this point you have three choices. The featured route uses the platelayers' path, which goes round Cressbrook and Litton tunnels. It is a grand path, with great views but some people find it rather exposed. In high wind or snowy and icy conditions it's best left alone. The other options are firstly to use the Monsal Trail and the now open tunnels or secondly to go down to Litton Mill and use the riverside path through Water cum Jolly Dale to Cressbrook Mill and there rejoin the featured route. The former has the merit of being virtually flat and dry. On the other hand you'll share the tunnels with cyclists who have never heard of giving audible warning of approach or the idea that reducing speed in a tunnel might be a good idea. Also you miss the views. The Litton Mill route is delightful and it too is flat, but there's extra ascent at the far end and if there's been a lot of rain the path can be flooded. On balance though, it's much nicer than walking through two tunnels. There's enough gloom in the world without seeking it out.

Be a platelayer

Go down the steps on the right, onto the Monsal Trail and follow the trail to the mouth of Litton tunnel. Having taken one look inside, bear left, up the rough path by the side of the line to a stile. A narrow path continues to climb up the slope, with increasingly good views both into the dale below and across the valley. Ignore the lower paths that run along the top edge of the limestone crags. These are climbers' paths and best avoided.

The path you are on is the one used by the railway company's platelayers to avoid walking through the tunnels (and if they avoided it, why should you do it we wonders? The tunnels were built for trains not walkers).

The path levels out at some small caves and then wriggles its way around the first bluff with a bird's eye view of Litton Mill far below. Once round the hill the path begins to descend slightly. Soon you come to the revegetated spoil heaps that came from Litton tunnel. The main path keeps to the right of these, to pass over Litton tunnel mouth and continue above but alongside the railway line. It is possible to descend through the spoil heaps to the Trail and continue from there through the next tunnel if you have a mind.

Continuing above the railway line you now reach Cressbrook tunnel mouth. The platelayers' path climbs away from the tunnel again and, as with the previous section, there are climbers' paths along the tops of the crags. Avoid these and keep high. There's a grand view across to Cressbrook village and in particular to Cressbrook Hall. Indeed, this is probably the best vantage point from which to see the hall. The path rounds the bluff and now Cressbrook Mill comes into view. As with the view of Litton Mill previously you get a bird's eye view of this superb building.

The path now descends gently to join the former route of the Monsal Trail and the route up from Water cum Jolly Dale. Continue along this path, which now runs virtually level to join the trail at the eastern portal of Litton tunnel.

Turn left here and follow the trail through Monsal Dale station. The railway station in Monsal Dale opened in 1866, to serve the villages of Upperdale and Cressbrook, along with the cotton mills. The 'down' line and platform were built on a shelf carved in the rock face, whilst the 'up' was built on wooden trestles over the hillside. It closed in 1959, and nothing now remains of the timber buildings, but the "down" line platform remains in situ.

Go back over Monsal Viaduct, then turn left and retrace your steps back up to Monsal Head and the Stables Bar for a well-earned glass of ale.

Walk 18. Monyash

The Route	Monyash, Bagshaw Dale, Lathkill Dale, Cales Dale, One Ash Grange Farm, Fern Dale, Monyash
Distance	4.1 miles (6.6 km). 732 feet of ascent (225 metres). Allow 2½ to 3 hours
Grade	Easy
Start	The Bull's Head, Monyash Village Green. Map reference: 150666
Map	OS Explorer OL24 The Peak District, White Peak Area
How to get there by bus	There's a useful Hulley's 178 from Bakewell on Mondays-Saturdays with an additional bus 177 on Saturdays and the High Peak 58 Macclesfield to Chatsworth bus on Sundays. They stop by the village green and pub
How to get there by car	Monyash is on the B5055 between the Ashbourne and Buxton road (A515)and Bakewell. There's limited car parking in the centre of the village and a small car park on the road to Flagg

The Pub

The Bull's Head

The Bull's Head (tel: 01629 812372) is a solid looking stone building dating from the 17th century. This is a long standing favourite of walkers and on a summer's day you see ramblers sitting on the seats outside overlooking the village green or, at other times, rows of boots stacked up near to the door. Please cover muddy boots or remove them when the weather is not so good. The pub remains very traditional; it is essentially in two parts. There's a long bar, serving Burton Ale and a local beer. Next to it is the games area with a pool table for the sport minded. The other area is given over as a dining room, which is more comfortable. The pub has a large fireplace adorned with an impressive coat of arms. The traditional furniture, ornaments and pictures all add to the atmosphere.

Lathkill Dale, Cales Dale junction

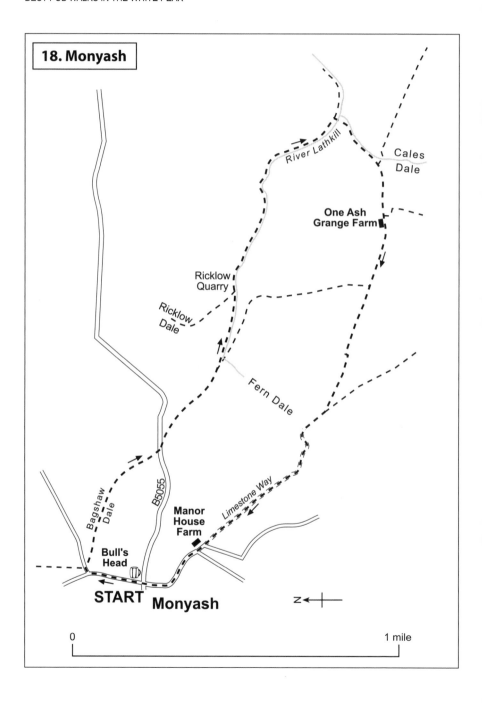

18. Monyash

River Lathkill

Cales Dale

One Ash Grange Farm

Ricklow Quarry

Ricklow Dale

Fern Dale

Bagshaw Dale

B5055

Limestone Way

Manor House Farm

Bull's Head

START Monyash

N

0   1 mile

The pub is open from 12 noon until 3pm, Monday to Thursday, and from 6.30pm in the evening. On Friday, Saturday and Sunday it is open all day. Food is usually served from noon until 2pm and from 6.30pm to 9pm. Food is also served all day at the weekends from noon until about 9pm. This is a very good pub to adjourn to after the walk!

This pub featured in the first edition of this book. Indeed a picture of it graced the front cover. No sooner had the book been printed than the pub name altered to "The Hobbit". When the book was reprinted with the altered name, lo and behold the pub name changed back again to the "Bull's Head". So it has remained. Hopefully the fact that the book is being reprinted again will not be an excuse for The Bull's Head to undergo yet another metamorphosis.

For early birds who like a breakfast before they walk there's also The Old Smithy (it was a blacksmith's) next door. Located by the village green, it has a tradition of offering breakfasts but there's much more nowadays with tasty morsels (locally sourced) on offer throughout the day for cyclists, walkers and villagers. There's also a beer on tap from Peak Ales located at Chatsworth!

The Walk

Monyash
Monyash is a deceptive sort of place, for it looks as if it has been primarily engaged in agriculture for its entire existence. This is only partly true, for in earlier times it was the centre for local lead mining, so much so that it had its own Barmote Court, similar to those found elsewhere in the Peak District. The area is known for its meres, small ponds formed on beds of clay and refreshed by limestone water springs. One of these still exists near to the green and is enclosed by a wall, presumably built at one time to keep animals out. The church spire is often reflected in the mere's calm waters. The church is a delightful building much restored throughout the ages.

Start the walk from the entrance to the Bull's Head on the village green. The village green retains the stem of the old cross and this was the site of a local market dating from a charter granted in 1340. Go right and walk past the Smithy tea-room and bistro and right again to walk along Chapel Street. Walk by the Methodist chapel dating from 1888, although Monyash also had a very strong Quaker community. Walk along the street to the end of the village.

Bagshaw Dale
Turn right at the junction for Sheldon and then go right again beneath a tree and through two gap stiles in close succession. This is Bagshaw Dale and the

path is clearly defined. Go through small gates, a gateway and two step stiles as you make your way down the shallow dale. The path becomes a track, passing barns and huts where horses are kept and this can be very muddy and there are often piles of manure too. So, tread carefully. Cut left at the road.

Ricklow Quarry

Cross over the main road, go through the gate and continue down the dale. There are three more gates on the way down the dale. After the 1st is an interpretation board. Between the 2nd and 3rd gates, a track diverges slightly to the right; do not to take this one but continue downhill. After the 3rd gate, the path narrows and leads downhill to a step stile. The path then passes through a deep, boulder-filled section, passing by the old Ricklow Quarry on the left. It is an eerie place. Nearby is Parson's Tor, so named because a local vicar from Monyash plunged to his death here in 1776. The path enters a nature reserve. This is a designated Natura 2000 site reflecting that this is one of the finest limestone valleys. Lathkill Dale is also known for its crystal clear waters, though nowadays you will be fortunate indeed to see any water this far up the dale. Continue alongside the drystone wall and fence down the valley, almost silent when there are few people around.

Cales Dale

You will pass Lathkill Head Cave on your right. This is the source of the River Lathkill in winter months. It is an impressive sight when in flow, usually after heavy rain. About 500 yards further down the dale (460 metres), you then come to a point where Cales Dale and Lathkill Dale join. Turn right and go across the footbridge. If there's water in the stream, keep a sharp look out for dippers. A well-walked path leads up Cales Dale, initially quite a steep ascent. You soon reach a junction of paths at the start of the climb beneath the limestone wall. Take the right hand path, signed with a fingerpost to Cales Dale and One Ash Grange.

Go right, climbing out of the dale to cross a stile and then walk through a wide green gap. Walk ahead to the farm and head for the steps between the barns. The path joins a track, which, after passing the Old Ash Grange Farm house, curves left and then right before continuing ahead. At the end, this track bears right then gives out through a gateway into a large field. Go left here, the finger post indicates Monyash, and now keep company with the wall on the left.

In the corner of the field go left over a stile and then turn right. Monyash village comes into sight. Keep ahead towards the village, passing through a squeezer stile and gate then through another by a broken wall. Continue ahead again, through a third stile at the bottom of a field into the top of Fern Dale, another former lead mining area. Go slightly right across the field to cross a stone stile by a signpost. Go left into a walled green lane. This leads back into the village. Continue ahead on the road to the village green and a well-earned break.

Walk 19. Rowsley and Stanton in Peak

The Route	Rowsley, Stanton Woodhouse, Endcliffe and Lees Cross quarries, Grey's tower, Cork Stone, Nine Ladies, Stanton in Peak, Congreave, Rowsley
Distance	6.7 miles (10.8 km). 1186 feet of ascent, (362 metres). Allow 3 to 3½ hours exclusive of stops
Grade	Moderate, with a number of climbs
Start	Rowsley (Station Close car park). Map reference: 258659
Map	OS Explorer OL24 The Peak District, White Peak Area
How to get there by bus	Daily bus services from Bakewell, Buxton, Derby, Manchester, Matlock and Sheffield. The stops are either just outside the former station, by The Peacock Hotel in the village, or at the junction with the Chatsworth road
How to get there by car	From the north-west and from the south follow A6 to Rowsley. The car park is on the south side of the road just east of The Grouse and Claret pub. It is not well signed, but it is free (at present). From Sheffield or Chesterfield come via Baslow, then A619, B6012 through Chatsworth Park and Beeley to the A6 at Rowsley. Turn right at A6 and the car park is about 100m on the left
How to get there by train	The nearest railway station is Rowsley South, on Peak Rail's line. This is about 1 mile (1.6 km) south of the starting point of the walk and is only served by seasonal trains from Matlock at present. Hopefully, during the currency of this book the Derby-Matlock service will be extended to Rowsley South. There's a footpath link from the station to Rowsley village

The Pub

The Flying Childers

Every now and then one comes across a really interesting pub name, something out of the ordinary. The Flying Childers is one such name and one cannot help but be intrigued as to its origin. The unusual name relates to the 4th Duke of Devonshire's favourite racehorse, which was a formidable challenger at any racecourse and apparently was never beaten. The horse was born in 1715 and died at Chatsworth in 1741. In the pub, a description of the horse states that its prize money was in the region of £20000 – an enormous sum in the 18th century. In his prime Flying Childers was reputedly able to cover 82 feet in a second, 25 feet in a single stride and leap 30 feet carrying a man! Quite a horse!

The pub dates from the 18th century when four cottages were combined. The pub (and much of Stanton) is owned by the Thornhill family of Stanton Estate and the letters "WPT" above the door (and over the doors of many of the cottages in the village), stand for William Pole Thornhill. The Flying Childers at Stanton in Peak (tel: 01629 636333) is a traditional pub in the heart of the Peak District. The landlord welcomes walkers, many of whom come to this particular part of the Peak not only to walk the moors but also visit the pub.

The public bar has a number of settles nestled near to the fireplace and is a reminder of what many rural public houses used to be like. Its simplicity is refreshing. There's also a lounge with more comfortable seating for those who like to relax a bit more. Families are welcome in the lounge bar, and there's a small beer garden to the rear.

This pub is renowned as a first class local and good all round pub for those who like good beer. Wells Bombardier is the regular ale plus two changing guest ales. These are usually from small local breweries but also some from further afield.

Opening times are; Monday and Tuesday 7- 11pm; Wednesday, Thursday, Friday 12 - 2pm 7- 11pm;

Saturday and Sunday 12 - 3pm 7- 11pm; Bank Holiday Mondays open lunchtimes 12 - 3pm. Light snacks are served (at lunchtime only) between 12 noon and 2pm. (Closed on Monday and Tuesday lunchtimes).

The Walk
Rowsley to Stanton Woodhouse

From the car park, turn left along the A6 and follow the main road into the village, passing over the Derwent. At the junction in the middle of the village, go left, following the signs to Caudwell's Mill. Pass the entrance to the mill car park and continue along the lane, crossing the River Wye.

At the junction by the playing fields go straight on, up the road marked as Private. It is a public footpath. The first part of this lane is delightfully flat, but you can just see Grey's Tower peeking above the trees on top of the hill to your right. This gives you a fair idea of the climb ahead. Looking to the right you can make out the medieval ridge and furrow marks in the fields. Where the lane forks, keep right and soon the climb begins. Fear not, it is very gradual and you will be surprised how rapidly you gain height. The lane passes through a wood, some of which has recently been felled and replanted. When you emerge there's a grand view down the valley to Riber Castle perched on its hilltop. Keep your eyes peeled for a footpath sign on the right. Go over the stile and follow the field edge to a gate that leads you back onto the lane you have just left, but at the top of an S bend. (There doesn't seem to be any reason why you need to use this path. You could continue up the lane and follow the footpath sign at the S bend). Continue along the lane, up into Stanton Woodhouse. This is a delightful little hamlet with some very fine buildings, including the hall (on your left as you pass through the hamlet), which is a basic 16th century house with many subsequent, but very tasteful additions.

Go through the hamlet and through the gate at the far end, to emerge into open fields. The lane degenerates into a cart-track, which swings gently left and then right, up the hillside. For railway enthusiasts, there's a bird's eye view of Peak Rail's Rowsley engine shed and sidings down to the left.

Still climbing, you pass a large clump of rhododendrons on the left. Go through the left-hand gate and where the track forks, almost imperceptibly, you keep left, still heading uphill. The path is not obvious underfoot at this point, but it soon becomes so as you reach Endcliffe Quarry site.

Eco-warrior encampment

There was a longstanding dispute relating to an application to reopen this quarry and Lees Cross quarry, which lies to your right. As a result of this, the two quarry sites were "colonised" by eco-warriors and when this walk was originally recce'd the next section passed through their encampment. The matter has now been resolved and the eco-warrior colony has moved away. There's no doubt that, from a visual point of view, reopening the quarries would be an eyesore and what could have happened here will be seen later in the walk. Continue along the path with the precipitous drop into the quarry on your left. Fortunately this is fenced off. The path forks as you near the road, so bear right and at the road turn right. Follow the road uphill for a short

Millstone in Lees Cross quarry

distance until you reach a track on the left, signposted as a public footpath. This leads up into Lees Cross Quarry site. Following the waymarks, skirt to the left of the ruined buildings and follow the broad, well-used path to a Y-junction. This is the boundary of National Trust land and there was once a sign here to tell you so. A broad track leads off left and a similar track goes right. If you are doing this walk in winter you will see Grey's Tower up on the hilltop through the bare trees. A narrow, steep path scales the hillside and comes out right by the tower, but this is not recommended and the way marked path clearly points to the right. Follow the right-hand path, which passes through Lees Cross quarries and is way marked in various places. This was also part of the eco-warrior camp, but the encampment and defence systems have been dismantled and it is difficult to envisage what it was like. The path twists and turns through the quarry site, now totally overgrown with mature trees. Look out for a big pit quarry on your left. Keep any small children well under control. See if you can spot the initials and dates carved in the main rock face. The dates all seem to be during the 1st World War. Just beyond this quarry there's a curious length of double stone kerbing in the centre of the path. Any offers as to its purpose? Eventually the path swings left and joins another coming up from the right. You are now on the edge of Stanton Moor.

Stanton Moor, Grey's Tower and the Cork Stone

Follow the path along the edge of the moor and along the top edge of Lees Cross quarry. The views over the Derwent valley are superb, but often hidden by trees. You soon come to Grey's Tower. This was erected to commemorate the passing of the 1832 Reform Act by Earl Grey's government. It was positioned prominently overlooking the Derwent valley so that it would serve as a reminder to the then Duke of Devonshire, who had opposed the reform. Unfortunately the tower cannot be climbed nowadays.

Go over the stile just behind the tower and take the left-hand path. (If time is running short, you can go right here. The path will take you direct to the Nine Ladies, where you can rejoin this walk description.) Follow the path across the moor, a delightful stroll. After about 800 yards (750m) the path forks. Carry straight on, heading towards an information panel which you will see ahead. This describes the use of the various tracks on the moor. Turn right here, skirting a large rhododendron bush and soon joining another path coming in from your right. You are now on the south edge of the moor, overlooking Winster. Ahead and to the left is a mound of fresh quarry spoil, from Birchover quarry – a salutary reminder of what Lees Cross and Endcliffe could have looked like had extraction recommenced. On the far horizon the

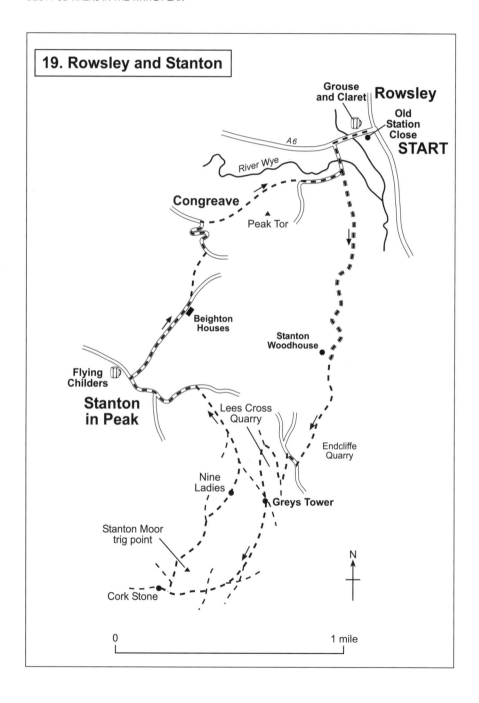

19. Rowsley and Stanton

Grouse and Claret | **Rowsley**

Old Station Close

START

A 6

River Wye

Congreave

▲ Peak Tor

Beighton Houses

Stanton Woodhouse

Flying Childers

Stanton in Peak

Lees Cross Quarry

Endcliffe Quarry

Nine Ladies

Greys Tower

Stanton Moor trig point

Cork Stone

N

0   1 mile

Cork Stone, Stanton Moor

curious looking tuft of trees marks Minninglow. This is one of the most prominent landmarks in the White Peak and it is amazing from how many vantage points it can be seen. At the major crossing of paths go straight on, soon topping the rise. There in front is the Cork Stone, which takes its name from its champagne cork shape. There are footholds and iron hand holds to help you get to the top. The top has its own round "washing up bowl". Most people who are at all young at heart will want to "have a go" at climbing the stone. It is not difficult in ascent, but there's not much room on top and it looks much higher from up there than it did from the bottom. Descent is rather more difficult. You have been warned and the authors take no responsibility for anyone deciding to attempt the climb.

A "trig" point and Nine Ladies

At the junction of paths by the Cork Stone, go right. The path immediately splits again, into three possible routes. Take the middle way, with the tip of Stanton Moor television mast as a guidepost. You are soon on top of the moor again. In a very short while you will see the summit of the moor to your right. This is marked by a "trig" point of white concrete, denoting a height of 323 metres, which sounded much better in English as 1050 feet. You can visit the trig point if you wish, otherwise continue along the well-blazed path, noting more old quarry working on the left, but also admiring the extensive view towards Bakewell. The path now enters an area of birch scrub and you will spot a fence ahead and to your left. This fringes more old quarry workings. The path wriggles its way through the birch wood until it reaches a corner of the fence and forks. The more obvious route, to the right, is the one you want and up a short rise, through the trees you reach the Nine Ladies stone circle.

Various tales are told of the origins of these stones, the most picturesque being that they were nine maidens who were turned to stone for dancing on a Sunday. The wicked person whose fiddle playing beguiled them into this sin was also turned to stone, hence the King Stone, a short distance away from the nine. In broad daylight there's no mystery about the stones, but when you come across them through the trees, with fog swirling about and the light dimming, it is a different matter. There are still tales of "strange goings-on" at the stones at times. For a more factual description, you could always rely on the information panel that has thoughtfully been provided.

Walk past the circle and bear left onto a broad track. This is then followed through a series of gates and stiles until you reach the end of the moor and enter open fields. A raised causeway leads across the fields to the road, where you turn left.

A gallop down to the Flying Childers

When you reach the top of the hill you have a choice. You can turn right, through the wood and go down a rough path to emerge at Beighton House or you can follow the lane down into Stanton in Peak. The former avoids road walking, but it also misses out an excellent pub. Decision made, go down the road, taking care as it is narrow and there's neither footway nor verge. As you descend, you pass the Wesleyan chapel on the right. This dates from 1829. At the "main" road, go right, still downhill, and again there's no footway. Buses for Bakewell and Matlock stop by the playground. At the next junction the main road continues downhill to the Flying Childers pub. Thirst satisfied, retrace your steps to this road junction and turn left along the lane.

And so to Rowsley

The lane is almost level and affords excellent views across the valley to Over Haddon, Youlgreave, Bakewell, Manners Wood and Haddon Hall. The view of Haddon Hall is most unusual and you certainly see more of the hall from this vantage point than from almost any other. (Just before Beighton Houses, the footpath short cut referred to earlier, comes in from the right). Just beyond Beighton Houses there's a most unusual viewing platform on the left: a half-circle, walled, stone platform complete with seat. This is an ideal place to sit and admire the view. Just beyond the viewpoint there's a sign-posted stile/gate on the left. Go over this and down the flight of steps into the field. Bear right and descend quite steeply, taking care in wet weather, as the grass is slippery. The exit stile/gate is obvious. Thereafter you follow the wall/hedge on the right down to a stile and gate, which disgorges onto a narrow lane. Turn left here and walk down the lane to the hamlet of Congreave.

The lane swings through a double zigzag. It is very narrow approaching the lowest bend and there's no verge, so be alert. Fortunately there's little traffic on this road, and what there's usually proceeds quite slowly because of the gradient and the bends. At the second left-hand bend, there's a footpath sign on the right. Go along the track beside Dove House Farm, to a gate into open fields. Contour right, with a view across to Haddon and Calton. The path rounds the nose of the hill and then descends to a stile and stream by a small wood. Once over the stream, go right, through a stile/gate and up through the wood to another stile, leading into fields. Bear slightly right, making for the bank and ditch surrounding Peak Tor. From here you can see the water supply arrangements for Caudwell's Mill. When you reach the bank and ditch, bear left and follow the track running alongside it. The bank and ditch soon bear away to the right, but the path continues to descend to a stile and gate near the river. Here you join the road. Continue beside the river to Rowsley, crossing the Wye and Derwent again and thus arriving back at the car park or bus stops.

Walk 20.Taddington

The Route	Taddington, Over Wheal, Deep Dale, Taddington Fields, and Taddington
Distance	5.2 miles (8.4 km). 876 feet of ascent (270 metres). Allow 2½ to 3 hours exclusive of stops
Grade	Easy walk with a small number of climbs
Start	The Queens Arms, Taddington. Map reference: 144711
Map	OS Explorer OL24 The Peak District, White Peak Area
How to get there by bus	Taddington is served by the daily High Peak TP bus between Manchester, Buxton, Bakewell, Matlock and Derby, which runs at a regular hourly frequency during the day
How to get there by car	The village is signed off the A6 road. There's a limited on-street parking in the village

The Pub

The Queen's Arms

The Queens Arms (tel: 01298 85245) has always been a popular calling point for ramblers over the years. The Queens has been a pub since 1736 and is said to have two resident ghosts: a little black dog and a young girl. On entering the pub there's a small bar to the left which now doubles as a pool room and village shop. Most people head for the larger L-shaped bar on the right. In this room there's a large attractive fireplace with a lovely warm fire in the winter and it is very spacious given that there's plenty of traditional seating away from the bar.

The Queens sells a range of cask beers, usually including several local brews e.g. from the Buxton and Barnsley breweries. It is open from 12 noon until 11pm every day (10.30pm on Sundays). Food is usually available at all opening times and on Sundays lunch/dinner is available from 12 noon until 9pm. To sum up, this is a great community pub, which welcomes walkers. Families and dogs (on a lead) are also welcome. There's limited seating outside.

The Walk

Find your way out of Taddington

The village of Taddington is best described as one long main street lined with delightful roadside cottages. It is criss-crossed by tracks and paths leading to other dwellings, barns or the open countryside. The mediaeval church is much larger than one would expect for a village this size, a reflection of Taddington's former prosperity as a wool trading area. There are several pre-historic burial mounds in the area, the most dramatic being the Five Wells Tumulus on the moor between Taddington and Chelmorton.

With your back to the entrance to Queens Arms, turn left and walk through the lower end of the village until the road bends. There are often geese and ducks wandering around this part and thankfully the road is quieter nowadays. Take the right hand fork and as this narrower road bends left, go right, by a barn and cottages, up a narrow track. This green lane rises up the hillside away from the village, soon reaching a junction. Go left here and climb gently up the hillside to join another walled track at the top, coming in from the right. Go left to follow this ahead to a road.

Over Wheal

Turn right to walk up the road, which rises through a sea of walled enclosures and with some remains of small-scale surface mining. The road levels and comes to a junction of tracks. It seems a million miles away from civilization now. Follow the track ahead as it descends to pass by Over Wheal Farm on the left. The track becomes a green lane and begins to make its way down into the upper end of Deep Dale. Ignore the stile and path to the left and continue to the valley bottom, where you go left through the gate and walk down the dale on the bridleway. The route is fairly clear on the ground as it follows the boundary wall, which divides the valley.

Deep Dale

Continue down the dale on the bridleway for about a mile (1.6 km) following the wall all the way. At a point where there's more scrub and there's a crag on the right, the path rises to the right and bends around to a junction. Go left here following the route signposted for White Lodge. Cross a step stile and go over a stream, which usually only runs in winter. The path bears right, passing through wet ground into a pasture, but be vigilant here for you are looking for a path on the left that is signposted to Taddington. It climbs up the hillside in a zig-zag fashion between hawthorn and elderberry. Cross a stile and continue ahead, still climbing and thus reach a gap stile on the left.

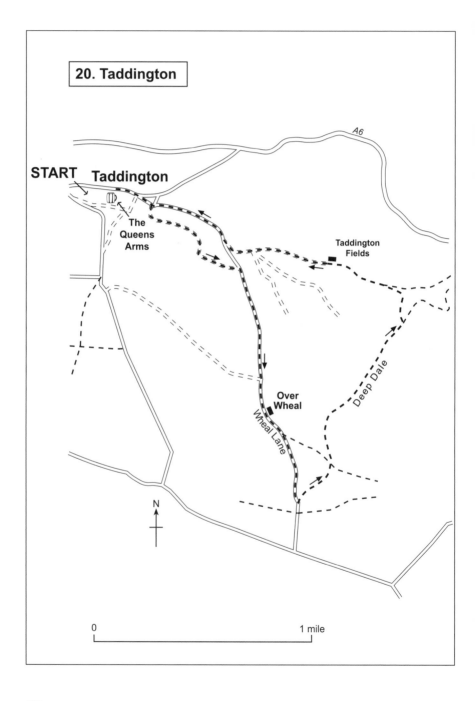

20. Taddington

START Taddington

The
Queens
Arms

A6

Taddington
Fields

Deep Dale

Over
Wheal

Wheal Lane

N

0   1 mile

Go through this and turn right to climb again. The path comes to a corner of a round drystone wall. Keep right here to follow the wall up to a step stile. Taddington Field Farm is to your right. Go over the step stile and keep right, heading towards the buildings. Proceed through a small gate. Then keep left to join a road leading away from the farm.

This track is a continuous steady climb. It passes Lodley View and then continues to a junction with a road. But beforehand, cut right along a short green lane referred to as a restricted byway. This drops down to a lane. Go down the lane, back into

The lane to Taddington

Taddington. At the main street, go up through the village and you will find the Queens Arms on the right. The bus stop (either direction-so stand opposite more or less for Buxton) is just before you reach the pub.

Walk 21. Thorpe

The Route	Thorpe, Spend Lane, Pike House, Tissington, Bassett Wood Farm, Fenny Bentley, and Thorpe
Distance	4¾ miles (7.7 km). 791 feet of ascent, (243 metres). Allow 2½ to 3 hours exclusive of stops
Grade	Easy with a few climbs
Start	The Dog and Partridge, Thorpe. Map reference: 164505
Map	OS Explorer OL24 The Peak District, White Peak Area
How to get there by bus	There's a daily bus service, High Peak bus 442, from Ashbourne and Buxton, which sets down by the Dog and Partridge pub
How to get there by car	Travel on the A515 from Ashbourne or Buxton. Thorpe is signposted from the A515 at Tissington Gates. Narlows Car Park is on the right just before the Dog and Partridge road junction

The Pub

Coach and Horses

The main pub on this walk is the Coach and Horses at Fenny Bentley (tel: 01335 350246). This 17th century coaching inn makes for a good mid walk stopping point and there are seats outside for summer days. Step inside the front door into the bar, with a flagstone floor, low beams and brasses. In the winter the Coalbrookdale wood burner warms the place to perfection. Beyond the bar is a restaurant area specifically for those who wish to dine and the inn likes to use local produce wherever possible.

The Coach and Horses has a stock beer, Marston's Pedigree. This is supplemented by offerings from various local breweries, e.g. Blue Monkey, Derby and Whim. The beer is on good form in this well run hostelry that welcomes walkers. The pub is open from 11 onwards on Mondays to Saturdays and from 12 noon until 1030pm on Sundays.

The Walk

Start from outside the Dog and Partridge pub. This stands at a crossroads away from the main village of Thorpe. You might have expected it to have been closer to the railway station. The explanation lies in the coaching era. It stands at the crossroads of what were two important turnpike roads. The east to west route was part of a road from the Potteries to Bakewell; the potters required 'chert' from Bakewell to use in the glazing process. The north to south route was part of the original Buxton to Ashbourne turnpike. This one-time coaching inn, with its stables behind, has been host to many a saddle-sore traveller in decades gone by.

With your back to the front entrance of the Dog and Partridge, go left to cross the main road and then ahead up Spend Lane. The importance of the lane in past times becomes apparent after a while given the width between the boundary walls. This road was turnpiked in 1738 but it was most probably upgraded from an ancient packhorse way before this time, following the high ground across the Peaks. The route was also described in the 1676 edition of Izaak Walton's 'Compleat Angler' where Charles Cotton tells the tale of a journey he made to his home at Beresford Hall near Hartington. Turnpikes usually had a wall-to-wall width of forty feet and this is no exception. Fortunately, this is a very quiet road now. As you approach Pike House on the left, there's a fine view of Thorpe Cloud, the miniature mountain guarding the entrance to Dovedale. At the National Trust sign just beyond the house, go through the gateway and through open pastures, still climbing towards a summit. The view to the right takes in Tissington and the southern Peak. You will see on the left the long-abandoned quarry. The road continues ahead. On the left you will see an old building across the pastures, originating from the quarrying days. Below, to your right, are Hollington End Farm and the A515. The A515 was a turnpike road built in 1776, replacing the route you are on now!

Ridge and Furrow

Beyond the National Trust gateway, in approximately 200 yards/metres, you need to look for a double finger post on the right. You want the left-hand path. Head slightly left across the field to join a drystone wall and descend almost parallel to it. There are some stylish stone barns hereabouts, like the one on your left in the next field. Cross a stile and drop down to another stile on the left by a gate. Then walk across a narrow pasture and turn right. Then cross a stone step stile in the drystone wall as signposted. The ridge and furrow strips are very evident here, the remains of the medieval open field system of farming. Head slightly left across the enclosure before crossing a

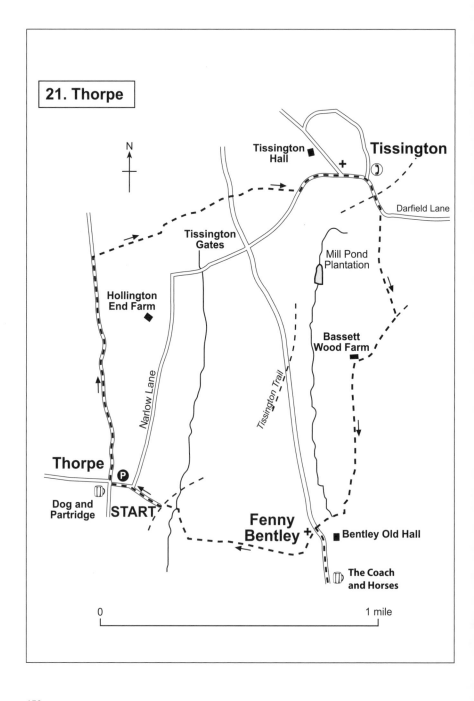

21. Thorpe

N

Tissington Hall

Tissington

Darfield Lane

Tissington Gates

Mill Pond Plantation

Hollington End Farm

Bassett Wood Farm

Narlow Lane

Tissington Trail

Thorpe

P

Dog and Partridge

START

Fenny Bentley

Bentley Old Hall

The Coach and Horses

0

1 mile

little bridge over a trickle of a brook and then reaching a gap stile. Now climb ahead to the main A515. Cross the road with extreme caution. This former turnpike is now a fast and busy road.

Tissington

Once safely ensconced in the parkland of Tissington Hall, head slightly left and just before the strip of woodland, go through the small gate by the barred gate. Now walk parallel to the arboretum, which is private. You soon reach the road to the village. Go left and walk into Tissington. If you have time, take a look round this delightful village. The Hall is sometimes open to visitors and in early spring the snowdrops are a picture. Tissington is famous for its well dressings and if you happen to be doing this walk when this event is on you should make a point of seeing the artistry that goes into this ancient craft. Leave the village past the duck pond, noting the various interpretation boards explaining the history and sights of the village. Your route rises up over the Tissington Trail, the former Ashbourne-Buxton railway. Go through a gateway to enter a grazing pasture. The road bends left but you cut right to go through a small gate by a barred gate in the hedge. In the next field head slightly left across it to the opposite hedge and then follow this ahead to a corner where you go through yet another small gate. Keep company with the hedge on the right and cross a stile to a road.

Fenny Bentley

Turn right and at the fork keep ahead for Bassett Wood Farm. As you approach the farm, there's a caravan field to the right and a barred gate where you will find a stile on the left before the farm buildings. Cross this stile and go ahead to cross another. Now head slightly right and you will catch sight of Fenny Bentley church. In the far right corner of the field, go through a gateway and walk down the hillside with a hedge to your right. There's a stile hidden in the bottom right corner beneath the hawthorn bush. Head slightly right, and aim for the field corner. Keep in the same direction to the next field corner where you will see a dwelling. Go right here and squeeze through a narrow gap stile by a gate. This leads onto a track, which runs down to the main road.

Go left for the Coach and Horses passing Bentley Old Hall.

You will need to retrace your steps back from the inn to this point, then cross the road and walk up stone steps by the lych gate into the churchyard, a truly rural idyll. Pass by the church on a tarmac path and exit by way of a gate at the other end. Go left along the road by houses. At the end of the housing, go right, to walk up a corralled section of path into the next field.

Keep ahead, now climbing more steeply to the brow of the hill. Now go through two small gates in a hedge and ahead again. At the next hedge go through another small gate and descend the hillside heading slightly right. Proceed through a gate in the hedge and continue until you reach the brook. Cross the footbridge and go through a gate before passing beneath the Tissington Trail. Continue up the track to reach the road and walk on to the Dog and Partridge. The bus stop for Ashbourne is across the road from the pub. Stand on the pub side for buses to Buxton.

Dog and Partridge, Thorpe

Walk 22. Tissington

The Route	Tissington church, Bletch Brook, Parwich, Parwich Lees, Tissington Trail
Distance	5¼ miles (8.5 km). 802 feet of ascent (247 metres). Allow 2½ to 3 hours exclusive of stops
Grade	Mostly easy but with a few climbs which nudges it towards a moderate walk
Start	Tissington village green. Map reference: 176523
Map	OS Explorer OL24 The Peak District, White Peak Area
How to get there by bus	Tissington village is served by a daily service from Ashbourne and Buxton; it is the High Peak 42 bus. The bus runs approximately every two hours and drops you right in the village by the green. The daily High Peak 442 runs along the main A515 road and drops you at Tissington Gates-this is a daily service too. It is 10 minutes walk from the main road, through the gates into the village
How to get there by car	Tissington is signposted from the A515 Ashbourne to Buxton road. There's a car park at Tissington old railway station on the edge of the village, 2-3 minutes walk from the church

The Pub

The Sycamore

The Sycamore (tel: 01335 390212) at Parwich is a wonderful little village local, a 19th-century hostelry that is now a Robinson's pub, located opposite the village green. It has been a CAMRA Good Beer Guide entry for many years. Enter through the front door and this pub has a homely and pleasant feeling; you will find fires in winter months to warm up the coldest of feet. It still remains very much the village local, as this is one settlement that remains fairly isolated. There's also a small seating area outside the pub, which makes for a very nice spot on a summer's day. As much of the pub is carpeted you are requested to cover muddy boots. There's also a small village shop in the pub now.

The Sycamore, Parwich

The pub opening times are from 12 noon until 2pm on Monday to Friday. This is extended until 3pm at weekends. The pub usually opens at 7pm in the evening. Food is served from mid-day until 1.45pm (2pm at weekends) and from 7pm to 8.30pm in the evening. The beer on tap is from Robinson's brewery of Stockport, a long-standing independent company dating from the 1830s. Families are welcome.

The Walk

Leaving Tissington

The walk starts at the green in Tissington. The 17th-century hall and estate buildings make this one of the finest villages in the Peak District and it is particularly popular at well-dressing time, a custom which dates back to a blessing of the purity of the water in times of plague and pestilence. This attracts so many people that the centre of Tissington can look more like a supermarket car park than a quintessential English village green extolling the virtues of a bygone era. But you will soon leave it behind for more tranquil pastures.

Climb up from the road to enter the churchyard of this pretty parish church. Before the main entrance door there's a green path, which cuts to the right

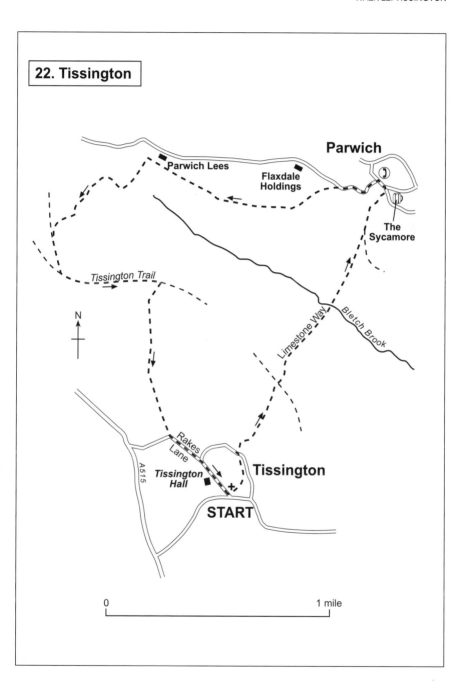

22. Tissington

Parwich

Parwich Lees

Flaxdale
Holdings

The
Sycamore

Tissington Trail

N

Limestone Way

Bletch Brook

Rakes
Lane

A515

Tissington
Hall

Tissington

START

0   1 mile

through the graveyard to a small gate in the boundary. In the first enclosure head slightly left and go through a wicket gate by a barred gate. Now proceed ahead in the next field and leave the dizziness of Tissington behind.

Bletch Brook

Cross the stile and then step across the lane to broach another stile. Both stiles are guarded by small gates, which is the fashion now. Go ahead across the field and exit onto another lane. Turn right on this lane, soon passing a dwelling. Follow the track over the Tissington Trail and cross a stile by a cattle grid. The track continues left to Shaw Farm but you need to cut right to descend the bank ahead, as indicated by the finger post. The view is good from here but it gets better. Drop down and ahead to cross a stone step stile, then onward to cross the footbridge over the Bletch Brook

Parwich

Now climb up the hillside, heading slightly left to cross a stile in the hedge at the top. Keep slightly left alongside a hedgerow to reach a gap stile in a hedge. There's a superb bird's eye view of Parwich in the valley from here. Your eye might at first be taken by the spire of the church, which can be seen for miles around. This is a settlement of Celtic origin mainly built of local limestone. The exception is the fine looking hall on the hillside opposite, a handsome Georgian building with terraced gardens. Continue slightly left down the hillside towards the village. Go through the gap stile and take the right-hand fork, cross a stile of sorts and walk on a path between a garden boundary and woodland strip. It can get a little squelchy here. This exits onto the village green, where families queue up to see what is happening in the duck pond. Beyond stands the Sycamore. It must be time for refreshment with all that climbing.

Parwich church

From the pub entrance turn right and walk on the road past the green and the stream. The church of St Peter stands to the right in the centre of the village. Keep ahead but at the next junction go left on a narrower road signposted for Alsop-en-le-Dale. The road bends as it leaves the village and begins to climb. Note the small cave on the left. Pass Brook Close Farm and then go next left through a small gate. Drop down to another gate by a barred gate. Head along the lower slope and then as you near the next boundary, turn left to climb a bank to locate a stile in the hedge. Cross this and head slightly left across the field before crossing a gap stile leading into a track.

Walk on to cross a stile. Ignore the path to the left, which incidentally is a much-loved and shorter route back to Tissington. However, we need more exercise so proceed ahead to go through a remnant of a gap stile and then head slightly left. Cross a gap stile in a hedge and proceed in a similar direction to another gap stile. Keep ahead to a wooden stile, then keep to the left of a barn by way of another gap stile.

Dry Gap

Now go slightly right, to cross a stile and then ahead to cross two more stiles, (ignore the one to the left) and enclosures before reaching the much-improved pastureland of Parwich Lees. Keep a line ahead (following the waymarks) through the parkland and you will see the house to your right, about 100 yards/metres from you. Please be considerate as you pass by. After this point the field dips and you will find a stile leading onto a track. Go left here and follow the track as it bends right and left to pass through a gap. Turn left to walk up through the dry gap. This is one of the loveliest corners of the southern Peak District. The track follows the wall on the right up the shallow valley as it curves left to a gateway. Go through it and turn right, now keeping company with the drystone wall on the right. Before you reach a gap stile in this wall, follow the path as it curves left to climb away from the boundary. It is actually a meeting of paths. If you reach the hawthorn you have missed the junction!

Cross the field and stile and keep ahead to go under the old railway bridge. Once through, turn left to climb up the embankment to join the Tissington Trail at Newton Grange. Turn right and stroll along for about 400 yards/metres, dodging the bikes on a summer's day. Walk through the cutting and you will see the cross path about 100 yards/metres beyond. Go right over a stile. A path runs across the field, slightly right, to a wall. You then follow this upwards and it soon becomes a walled track for a short length. Continue ahead on a wide path through fields. There's further evidence of strip and furrow farming here possibly from the late mediaeval period.

Exit onto Rake Lane and turn left to return back to Tissington, where there are shops, a café and other places of interest, but alas, no pub.

Walk 23. Warslow

The Route	Warslow, Brownlow, Butterton, Swainsley Head, Warslow Brook, Villa Farm, Warslow
Distance	3.8 miles (6.2 km). 681 feet of ascent, (210 metres). Allow about 2½ hours exclusive of stops
Grade	Moderately easy with one hard climb
Start	The Greyhound in Warslow Village. Map reference: 086587
Map	OS Explorer OL24 The Peak District, White Peak Area
How to get there by bus	The village of Warslow is served by a daily bus, service 442, from Ashbourne, Hartington and Buxton – generally, every two-hours. The bus stop and shelter is at St Lawrence View and it is a one-minute walk to the pub. When you alight from the bus, which basically does a loop around the church, walk ahead to the junction (at the old post office) and turn left. Do not use the stop by the pub – the bus does not stop there. The demand responsive service, Moorlands Connect serves Warslow on Mondays to Saturdays, telephone 0300 1118003 for details
How to get there by car	Travel on the B5053 from Bottom House on the Leek to Ashbourne road or south from the A515 at Brierlow Bar near Buxton. The road passes through the village of Warslow. There's no specific place to park a car except some on-road spaces near to the church

The Pubs

The Greyhound (Warslow)

The Greyhound (tel: 01298 687017) at Warslow dates from 1750 and the stone building stands neatly back from the roadside at the top end of the village. It used to be called the Greyhound and Hare in earlier times. The pub has been refurbished to good effect in recent years and is much more welcoming than in years gone by. It is now a very pleasant place to have a beverage and food.

On the bar is a range of cask conditioned ales, usually London Pride and Pedigree, but also you'll find guest ale is often available. There's also a beer garden for sunny days. The Greyhound is open on Mondays and Tuesdays from 5pm onwards and Wednesdays and Thursdays lunchtimes and from 5pm. It is open all day Fridays to Sundays.

The Black Lion (Butterton)

The Black Lion (tel: 01538 304232) at Butterton is to be found mid-way on the walk. It is a lovely old inn, with the current building dating from 1782. This multi-roomed hostelry with its low beams and kitchen range is a very homely sort of place. It welcomes the walker and there's a range of guest beers on hand pull. Opening times (for winter months) is from 7pm Mondays-Fridays and 12-2 and from 7pm on Saturday. It is open all day on Sundays. However, these hours are extended in the summer.

The Black Lion, Butterton

The Walk

Warslow

Warslow is a quiet village, which has lost many of its local facilities in the past decade. It is a place that many pass through rather than stop, which is a pity. Nevertheless, the nucleus remains the parish church at the centre of the village. It has a number of William Morris windows and other interesting

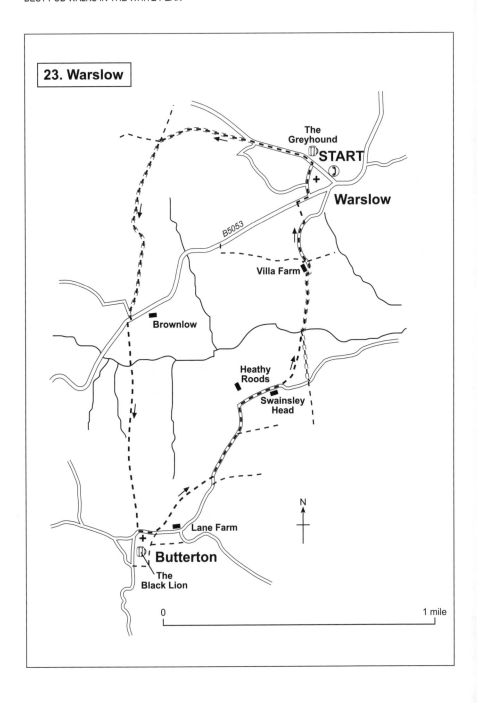

23. Warslow

features. There are also some interesting styles of stone buildings around the older part of the village.

With the entrance of the Greyhound pub behind you, turn right and walk alongside the road to pass by the school. At the edge of the village you'll see a road off to the left – ignore this one. Instead, take the second exit on the left, a track that is signposted, and passes a dwelling on the left. The track bends to the left and descends the hillside. You can see the spire of Butterton church in the distance and on a clear day you will also see the spire of Grindon church beyond.

Old green way

On reaching the end of the enclosed track the path continues ahead on what was a continuation of this old green way. Go over a stile and keeping the fence to your right, go over a step stile to the left of a barred gate, walking ahead at first but then towards an old barn. Go over a stile into the enclosure around the barn and pass to the right of the building to exit. In the next field, keep slightly left here, following the hedge on your left. Cross a drystone wall and descend to cross another stile in the hedge, to reach a road.

Go left here to the junction, then go right for twenty paces. Cross over to the left and climb a step stile to enter a field, then another in close succession. It is interesting to note that hedgerows are prevalent in this area rather than the traditional drystone walls. This is because you are not on limestone at this point. Walk ahead with a hedge to your left. The path then zigzags down between hawthorns on the right past a stone marker to the footbridge.

There follows something of a climb, so brace yourself. Ahead is a scarred edge with a long thin spine running between two shallow gullies. Most people cut to the right of these and make a fairly direct ascent up the hillside. There are no landmarks as such until the slope levels. Head slightly right and you will pass well to the right of the old barn. Cross the stile by the barred gate and continue ahead to come alongside a tree-lined green lane, passing through a gate and along a well-defined track.

Butterton

This exits onto a road by the church in Butterton. If you are calling at the Black Lion bear right, but otherwise go left along the road. Just beyond the perimeter of the churchyard look for a gap stile on the left to enter a field. Now head right and, in the next boundary hedge, there's a farm to your right. Once through, head for the far right-hand corner where a stile sits beneath a tree. Cross it and go ahead through a narrow enclosure. Ten paces on the left, go through another stile and then through a gap stile. Walk to the right through the next field to a stile by a barred gate. Keep ahead to the point where a gap stile exits onto a road.

There's more traffic on this lane than we would like, so be careful. Turn left and walk past the entrance to Heathy Roods Farm. The road begins to descend and passes Swainsley Head Farm on the right. Now look for the barn on the left. Your path enters the field over a stile by the barn. Pass to the right of the barn and drop down the hillside to go through a gate below and beyond the electricity pole. At the opposite end of the next field you reach the remains of an old trackway, now a bridleway. Join this and follow it down to the Warslow Brook.

At first it looks as if you have to wade through the stream, but just to the left is a fine footbridge. Once over, head slightly right up the hillside to rejoin the bridleway. Go

Butterton church

through the gate and walk up to another gate to a garden of a dwelling. The bridleway is ahead but you are invited to make a slight diversion left on a drive, which is less intrusive. This rejoins the bridleway and becomes a road, climbing up to the village. You can do this, or part way up, opposite a building cross a wooden stile identified by the remains of a small stone gap stile. Go ahead in the pasture to another gap stile and ahead to another under a tree and to a gap stile. The path comes out on the main road in Warslow. Go right and turn next left for the bus stop, shelter and pub.

Walk 24. Waterhouses

The Route	Waterhouses, The Manifold Way, Grindon, Deepdale Farm, Back o' th' Brook, Ford, Waterfall, Waterhouses
Distance	6.3 miles (10.2 km). 877 feet of ascent (270 metres). Allow 3 to 4 hours exclusive of stops
Grade	Moderate
Start	Ye Olde Crown Inn, Waterhouses. Map reference: 084502
Map	OS Explorer OL24 The Peak District, White Peak Area
How to get there by bus	There's a bus service daily 108 (Clowes on Mondays-Saturdays, TM Travel on Sundays) between Ashbourne and Leek, approximately two-hourly, and with onward connections to and from Derby, Macclesfield and Stoke. The demand responsive service, Moorlands Connect serves Waterhouses on Mondays to Saturdays, telephone 0300 1118003 for details
How to get there by car	Travel on the A523 from Ashbourne or Leek to Waterhouses. There's a car park, which is signed off the main road. It is located at the old railway station and there's a cycle hire centre and toilets there as well

The Pubs

The Red Lion (Waterfall)
The Red Lion in Waterfall (tel: 01538 308279) is a real survivor. It is located on one of the very quiet lanes which, along with the numerous paths threading in and out of the scattered properties, are a feature of this small community. This is not an old hostelry as it was probably built in the latter part of the 19th century, no doubt using stone quarried from nearby. The solid Victorian exterior of the hostelry, with its two bay windows, can be seen to good effect across the pasture from the parish church. There are seats outside the pub for those visiting during the summer months. It's a homely inn, offering, as it has always done, a meeting place for residents and visitors alike.

The Red Lion has for some years now offered two traditional cask ales from local or regional brewers. The Red Lion is open every evening from 6.30pm on Mondays to Fridays and all day at the weekends. Meals are served on Monday to Fridays from 6.30pm to 8.30pm but only at lunchtimes at the weekend. Families and walkers are welcome. However, as the pub is carpeted throughout, ramblers are requested to remove muddy boots.

Ye Olde Crown (Waterhouses)
Ye Olde Crown at Waterhouses is also a very friendly pub which is open at lunchtimes on Mondays to Fridays and all day at weekends. The pub often serves Marston's Pedigree cask beer.

The Walk

Into the land of vanishing rivers
Start from Ye Olde Crown in Waterhouses on the junction with the road to Cauldon. There's a village store almost next door if provisions are required for the walk. From Ye Olde Crown, cross the road and turn right to walk along the pavement through the village. The traffic on the A523 makes this a less than pleasurable experience. Keep glancing over the wall to your left at the River Hamps. It's often a case of "Now you see it; now you don't", because this river, like a number of others in the area, has a habit of vanishing underground in dry weather. In a few minutes you peel off left onto the Manifold Way. This long-standing walking and cycling route uses the trackbed of the old Leek and Manifold Light Railway, which closed in 1934. During the summer and at weekends the track is frequented by large numbers of cyclists but is still very useful for walkers seeking paths in the valley.

Cycle hire centre Waterhouses

Lea Farm
Follow the track for a mile (1.6 km) as far as Lea Farm, crossing over the River Hamps twice. This section will take you about 20-30 minutes. The landmarks are clear. You approach the second bridge over the river, or river bed, as it is

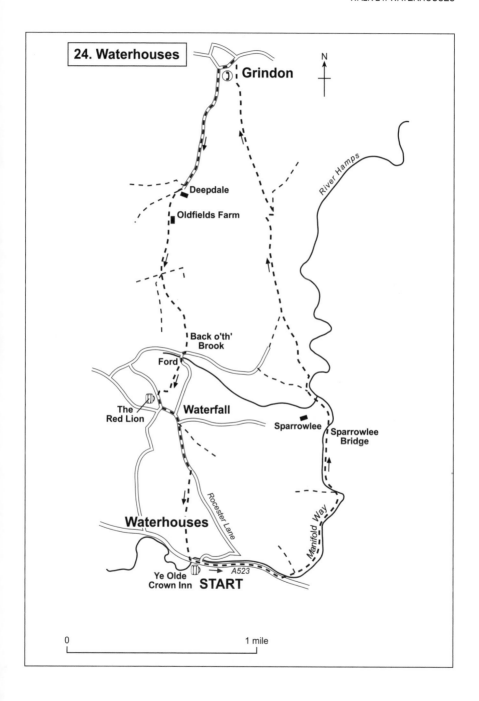

24. Waterhouses

Grindon

N

River Hamps

Deepdale

Oldfields Farm

Back o'th' Brook

Ford

The Red Lion

Waterfall

Sparrowlee

Sparrowlee Bridge

Rocester Lane

Manifold Way

Waterhouses

Ye Olde Crown Inn START

A523

0   1 mile

not always in water given the porous nature of the limestone. Once over this second bridge you should be able to see Sparrowlee Farm to your left up the hillside. Continue ahead and you will see a footbridge on the right leading to Lea Farm where refreshments are served. This is a delightful spot and deservedly popular with walkers and cyclists.

Be vigilant here, for your way is to the left, through a wicket gate opposite the footbridge, leading into a pasture. Once through go right. Walk on through two more gates and then right to cross a stile.

Once through, go right to walk through two more gates, then follow the track through a small wood to an opening into another field. Bear left uphill past a ruined building to a stile in the far left hand corner of the field. Follow the route to the right over another stile beside a wicket gate. Cross the field to another gate, keeping the hedge to your right. Once across, make your way to the left of the barn and to a gate located just beyond it. Follow the line of trees to another gate leading to a narrow tarmac lane.

For those seeking a shorter walk you can turn left along this road into Waterfall where you can pick up the longer walk at the paragraph headed 'Ford'.

Otherwise, there's still more climbing as you turn right to continue, onwards and upwards towards Grindon. The views are rewarding and when you need a rest simply take a look behind you to Throwley Moor and Mere Hill. The road leads to an isolated farmstead. Pass in front of the farmhouse and through the yard to reach a gate into a field. Go through the gate. This can be very muddy in winter.

Grindon and not a Cavalier in sight

The track runs parallel with a drystone wall on the left down to a gateway. Then the path zigzags up the hillside to the right and then left to another gate. Go through it and keep company with the drystone wall on the left, rising towards the village of Grindon. The name Grindon is said to be derived from 'Greendon' signifying a green hill. The village is readily identified by its conspicuous church spire, built in the 19th century in Gothic Revival style. The path leads to an old green lane that is followed to the outskirts of the village. Interestingly, the map shows a path adjacent to it, a sure sign that it was impassable on foot in earlier times, rutted no doubt by wagons. In wet weather the track is muddy, so it may be worth seeing if the adjacent path is still passable. At the fork keep left and then exit onto a road and into the village. Go left again and you will see a pinfold to your left and ahead a building that was the Cavalier pub until its closure in 2009.

Go left by the pinfold along a "No through road" to a scatter of dwellings known as Deepdale. Ignore the left fork at Manor Farm. Simply keep ahead until the narrow road passes Deepdale Farm and through to Old Fields Farm where your way is ahead by the farm buildings. The farmhouse is set back to your left. Just beyond the traditional 18th-century farmhouse, the track veers left through gateways. It then goes right to follow a drystone wall by outcrops and through a gate. It then descends slightly right, and beneath a disused quarry set back on the left, to the next field boundary, where you go through a gate. Remnants of the old track, Slade Lane, are to be seen on the ground as you keep company with the wall on the left, which curves slightly to the left. The track now becomes more obvious and after the next gate becomes a sunken way that descends to a few houses at Back o' th' Brook.

Rundle Stone, Grindon

Ford

The name, no doubt, identifies the importance of the brook as a boundary between this small settlement and the remainder of the township of Waterfall. Go right on the road and then at the junction go left across the ford. You'll have to step gingerly across the stepping-stones after rainfall, but otherwise the brook is little more than a trickle here. As the road curves left, pause a moment to seek out a path off to the right, through bushes, to a gap stile in the boundary here. Once in the field, take a deep breath and climb steadfastly up the hillside, through the gap stile to the churchyard. Before entering the churchyard take a look back at Waterfall Low, a wooded hilltop with burial tumuli, thought to date from Bronze Age times.

Waterfall church stands proudly on high ground in the heart of the community. The church dates originally from the 12th century but was much restored in the 19th century. It is a romantic setting with drystone walling richly covered in lichens and moss, stone barns and dwellings in various states of repair and numerous paths leading to narrow gap stiles from the same era. Please walk with care in the churchyard. Pass to the right of the church and then right again into an adjacent field. You will see the Red Lion ahead. Walk across the field heading to the left of the public house and you will exit onto the road by way of two squeeze stiles nestled by a stone barn. The Red Lion stands before you.

If not imbibing, then go left along the road to a junction. Go left here, but not immediately left at the pocket size green, which despite its size boasts stocks and an old water pump. Instead, you keep ahead to a junction immediately beyond the green and left here into Rocester Lane. Continue ahead, ignoring the two junctions to the left, and when the road begins to descend, opposite an entrance to a dwelling on the left, there's a stile and signpost on your right. Enter the field and the finger post indicates your way on a well-worn path, which runs through a series of enclosures to Waterhouses. There are some fine examples of stone gap stiles although they are cluttered with wire or wood in some

The Red Lion, Waterfall

cases. Follow the path to the final water meadow and the main road and turn left to walk back to Ye Olde Crown.

Walk 25. Wetton

The Route	Wetton, Thor's cave, Manifold Trail, Beeston Tor, Wetton
Distance	4 miles (6.5 km). 1168 feet of ascent, (356 metres). Allow 3 hours exclusive of stops
Grade	Moderate but with some steep descents and ascents, (plus potential wet feet)
Start	Ye Olde Royal Oak public house, Wetton. Map reference: 109554
Map	OS Explorer OL24 The Peak District, White Peak Area
How to get there by bus	The demand responsive service, Moorlands Connect serves Wetton on Mondays to Saturdays, telephone 0300 1118003 for details. Service 442 (Ashbourne-Buxton) is the nearest daily service, alight at Hulme End. Wetton is 2.75 miles (4.5 km) from Hulme End (plus a further 622 feet (190 metres) of ascent) or walk down the Manifold Trail to Thor's Cave (3.6 miles/5.8 km)
How to get there by car	Wetton is signed from Hulme End on the B5054 road from Hartington. After about 1.7 miles take a right turn (signed to Wetton) and follow this narrow lane to a T-junction in the village, opposite the Royal Oak. Turn left and follow the signs to the car park and toilet block at the SW edge of the village

The Pub

Ye Olde Royal Oak
Ye Olde Royal Oak (tel: 01335 310287) is a friendly pub, thought to date from the 1760 or possibly a little earlier. There are several cosy nooks around the bar, oak beams and a roaring fire which make it very homely. There's a mix of visitors and residents in this genuinely local English pub. Note the pictures on the wall of the prestigious world toe wrestling championships, which take

place here. Wetton is a charming village, at one time an agricultural centre but now the village is predominantly dormitory, with quite a few holiday cottages. The inn and the church stand at the centre of the community, side by side and this nucleus forms a conservation area.

On hand pull are Cumberland from Jennings, Black Sheep Bitter and Ruddles County (the latter is brewed by Greene King). Boot covers are provided for walkers and families are welcome. There's accommodation available including camping.

Ye Olde Royal Oak, Wetton

Opening Times: Monday and Tuesday closed (except Bank Holiday Mondays); Wednesday to Friday 12.00-2 pm and 7pm-11pm; Saturday and Sunday 12.00-2.30pm and 7pm-11pm

The pub is open every day during school holidays and all day Saturdays and Sundays. Food is served each day from noon to 2pm and from 7pm to 8.45 pm. Wherever possible, it is sourced locally and freshly cooked.

The Walk

Through Wetton village

From the car park, turn left and at the T-junction in the village turn right, soon reaching the Royal Oak. Resisting the temptation to imbibe at this stage, carry on past the pub and then go left again to go through the churchyard. The church is dedicated to St. Margaret and is well worth a look round. The path exits the churchyard alongside the village hall and here you turn left again to walk along the road to a junction. Keen students of the map will have realised that the lane you have just reached could have been accessed much quicker from the car park by turning right rather than left, but you'd have missed seeing the pub and the church. Bear right along the lane, but almost at once, a track branches left and is signed as a concessionary path to Thor's Cave. Walk along this pleasant walled track, with increasingly good views across the Manifold Valley towards Grindon, with the church spire being very obvious. The hillside facing you lies above Thor's Cave and the top of the cave can just be seen as you go down the track.

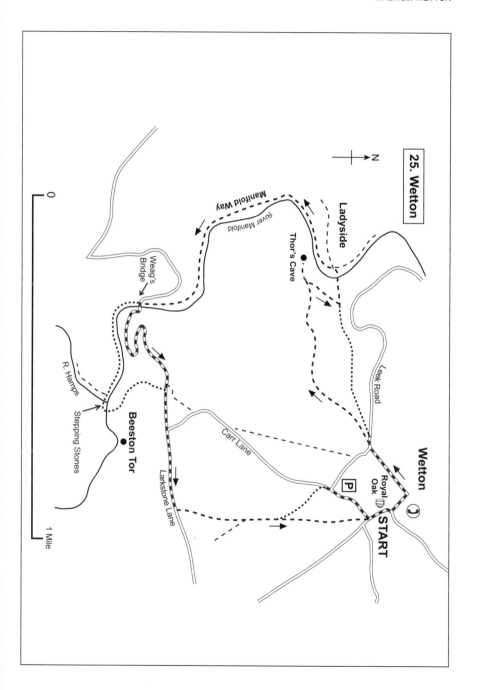

25. Wetton

Ladyside

Manifold Way

River Manifold

Thor's Cave

Weag's Bridge

R. Hamps

Stepping Stones

Beeston Tor

Carr Lane

Larkstone Lane

Leek Road

Wetton

Royal Oak

P

START

0 — 1 Mile

Thor's Cave

Go through a gate or over the adjacent stile and continue on the track until you reach a signpost directing you to the right. Go over another stile and down the field to a stile/gate. Here the path forks. Many turn left here and go to the top of the hill to admire the view of the Manifold, both north and south. The view extends much further however and takes in the hills beyond the River Trent, well to the south. Take great care if you do go up the hill because you will be on steep grass and slippery limestone and there's a near vertical plunge into the valley from the top. To visit the cave you must return to the junction of paths and now go left, initially down steps, then on a path, which leads unerringly to the cave. The entire experience is fairly exhilarating. This cave was apparently the home of prehistoric humans and the view from the entrance is magnificent. However, care is needed, because the floor of the cave is well-polished limestone and can be slippery when wet. A fall here would see you in the valley bottom rather quicker than you anticipated!

Retrace your steps for a short distance and then bear left down a well-built flight of steps which take you down to join a path coming down from Wetton. (If all you wanted to do was visit the cave, you can turn right here and go back up, through the wood and then across the field to reach the road, close to the point where the concession path took off). Turn left at the junction of paths, signposted to Ladyside, and go down to the valley bottom where you cross a footbridge over the Manifold, which may or may not be in water depending on the season.

Weag's Bridge or Beeston Tor's stepping-stones?

Join the Manifold Trail and turn left. The Trail was once a railway, the much lamented Leek and Manifold Light Railway, which for 30 years ran from Waterhouses to Hulme End and served precious little in between. It is probably true to say that the "line" now carries more people than it ever did when it was a railway. You need to be a bit wary if the trail is busy with bikes but it is a beautiful stretch. Look out for the rich flora and fauna in Ladyside Wood on your right. A gentle stroll of ½ mile (800 metres) leads to the car park at Weag's Bridge, though railway aficionados would call it Grindon station. At this point the Grindon-Wetton road crosses the valley. Here you have a choice.

For the less adventurous, or more sensible, go left here. Cross over Weag's Bridge, then through a gateway and over a cattle grid. You can stay on the road and climb the hillside, but those who are up for a serious climb should cut left up a path through bracken and thorn to a point further up the hillside, thus rejoining Larkstone Lane. Follow the road up to another cattle grid, at which point the adventurous walkers will rejoin you.

Beeston Tor

The alternative, more adventurous route is to continue down the Manifold Trail (that's the one with the "flying motor-bike" sign) until it bears away to the right, heading up the Hamps valley. Go left here onto the track and public footpath, which crosses the Hamps and then reaches a caravan site. Here you'll spot a curious wooden building. This was the tea room at Beeston Tor station. The tor rises dramatically to your left. A short distance further on, there's a waymarked gate on the left and a signpost directing you alongside the river to "The stepping stones". This is where the adventure comes in. If the river is in its dry state, there's no problem. If, on the other hand, it is in spate, or even moderately full, then the middle stepping-stones will be under water. Unlike the Dovedale stepping-stones, these stones have not fallen victim to the health and safety police, so they are rough limestone blocks, polished and slippery. You then have the decision to make, whether to venture the stones or retrace your steps back to Weag's Bridge. Discretion may be the better part of valour and you can always console yourself by having seen the remnants of the railway and the magnificent Beeston Tor. If you do get across the river, a good wide track slants upwards and the path emerges onto Larkstone Lane by the cattle grid. Turn right and go up the lane.

Larkstone Lane climbs to a T-junction with Carr Lane. Carry straight on, still on Larkstone Lane, until you reach the brow of the hill. Go left here, through a gap stile and head towards the barn standing prominently on the hillside, thus locating another squeezer stile in the first boundary wall. A step stile by a gateway leads into the small enclosure surrounding the barn. Keep to the right of the barn, but continue ahead. As you top the rise, Wetton comes into view and to your right is the trig point on Wetton Low. The path bears right across a large field, keeping to the left of the solitary tree. Head towards the midpoint of the wall forming the right-hand boundary.

If you are making for the car park, turn left just before the boundary wall and follow it down to the road, where you turn right.

If you are making for the village (and the pub), seek out a step stile in the wall and continue heading towards the village through a series of smaller fields with squeezer stiles. You come to a final small enclosure and then exit on a road at the edge of Wetton. Go right and then left at the junction to reach the Royal Oak.

Walk 26.Whatstandwell

The Route	Whatstandwell railway station, Crich Carr, Benthill, Crich, Crich Stand, Crich village, The Tors, Chadwick Nick, Crich Chase, Cromford canal
Distance	6.1 miles (9.8 km), 986 feet (301 metres) of ascent. Allow 3 to 3½ hours exclusive of stops
Grade	Moderate with one lengthy climb
Start	Whatstandwell station. Map reference: 333542
Map	OS Explorer OL24 The Peak District, White Peak Area
How to get there by bus	There are daily services along A6 from Manchester, Stockport, Buxton, Matlock and Derby (High Peak TP). Alight at the Derwent Hotel and join the walk at the canal bridge. There are daily services to Crich from Alfreton, Matlock and Ripley
How to get there by car	Whatstandwell station is signed just off A6 and (usually) has ample parking space. It is pay and display. There's also limited (free) off-street parking by the canal bridge just off the A6. Crich is signed off the A6 at Whatstandwell and off the A610 at Bull Bridge. There's limited on-street parking in Crich Market Place
How to get there by train	There's a daily service to Whatstandwell from Matlock, Derby and Nottingham

The Pub

Cliff Inn

Crich has no shortage of pubs but our favourite is The Cliff. The Cliff Inn (tel: 01773 852444) stands next to the Crich Tramway museum so as you can imagine it is more concerned with tram drivers calling in at the end of their shift than ramblers, but you can be assured of a friendly welcome. There are two bars, often buzzing with enthusiastic conversation about the latest developments at the museum, and you should allow time for a visit to this fascinating insight into the world of trams.

Opening times are; Monday to Friday 5pm till "late", Saturday and Sunday 12 noon till "late"

Food is served Tuesday to Friday 6pm to 9pm and 12 noon to 9 pm on Saturdays and Sundays. All food is locally sourced.

This was a Hardy and Hanson house so the beers are now from the Greene King Brewery, but the speciality is locally sourced real ales from breweries all over the Peak District and Derbyshire, all brewed with a 15-mile radius of The Cliff Inn! Recent offerings include beers from Ashbourne, Ashover, Bakewell, Chatsworth, Chesterfield, Derby, Eastwood, Glossop, Hartington, Ilkeston, Ripley and Shardlow. All in all, this is an impressive list. As the website so nicely puts it, "Please note, the availability of guest beers is entirely subject to the enthusiasm of our customers". Families are welcome, and so are dogs.

The Walk

Steps and Ginnels

From the station platform at Whatstandwell, cross the footbridge over the railway and the canal. (If you've got off the bus at The Derwent Hotel walk up the road towards Crich, turn right, onto the canal towpath and cross the canal by the footbridge from the railway station. The same applies if you've parked by the canal bridge). From the end of the canal footbridge, go up the ginnel to the road. At the road go right, and then immediately left, up Hindersitch Lane, climbing steadily. Look out for the curious metal gate on the right. The road bends left past an old chapel and continues to climb. At the fork in the road, by the seat, bear right up Glen Road – little more than a rough lane at this point. Where Glen Road finishes another ginnel continues straight ahead, to the right of the house called The Willows. This path emerges on another road opposite a water trough. Turn right and almost at once, look out for a signpost on your left. A lengthy flight of steep steps leads between houses, so up you go. At the top of this flight you cross a disused track and then go up another flight of steps to reach the access to Benthill Farm. Cross the driveway and go up more steps, through a stile and out into fields. Benthill Farm is just to your right and the path heads straight up the field to a stile. Here the path forks.

A heavenly guide?

Take the left-hand route, making for the spire of Crich Church, which can be seen peeping over the top of the hill. Crich Stand is prominent to the left – Derbyshire's only lighthouse. Pass through a stile and follow the wall on your right to another stile in the top right-hand corner. In the next field the wall is

Crich village and church

now on your left, again guiding you to the exit stile. Take a look back at this point for a magnificent view over the Derwent valley towards Wirksworth.

A mirage?
You will now notice Derby Assembly Rooms away to your left, but don't be alarmed. You have not gone badly off course. This is the old Assembly Room frontage that was re-erected at Crich Tramway museum to help create an authentic street scene.

Decisions, decisions
At this point the path again forks. Here it is decision time.

If you are heading for the tramway museum, the Cliff Inn and Crich Stand you need to bear left and soon join a path coming across the field from your right. Turn left and follow this path, which soon becomes a rough lane and emerges onto the main road, almost opposite The Cliff Inn. The tramway museum is well worth a visit, but make sure you've sufficient time to do it justice. Likewise Crich Stand is worth the extra ascent if only for the view, but if you do go to the Stand, spare a thought for the 13000 men of the Sherwood Foresters regiment who died in the two world wars and who are commemorated by this monument. The beacon light in the tower can be seen over a wide area of Derbyshire and Nottinghamshire, very fitting as the majority of men in the regiment came from these two counties.

Having imbibed, eaten, ridden on a tram, visited Crich Stand (or all four), go down the main road past the church to the Market Place. You can now skip the next two paragraphs.

If you are not visiting the tramway museum or the pub or Crich Stand, take the right-hand route, which makes a bee-line for the church. Note the bridge ahead. This carried the path over the former Crich Mineral Railway. At this point the line was originally a rope-worked incline, but in 1893 steam engines replaced the ropes. Don't go over the bridge, but turn right at the gateway, which is signposted.

Through Crich

The path crosses another field and thus reaches Wheatsheaf Lane. Carry on down the lane, bearing right where Jeffrey's Lane joins. Keep a look out on your left for the fine stone arched bridge, which is about all that remains here of the former railway. At the next road junction go left and descend to Crich market place.

Turn right, up Sandy Lane, passing the Baptist chapel on your left and then the former reading room dating from 1889. Ignore the first path on the left, but go along the second one, which leads past the Jubilee trees, planted to commemorate the golden and diamond jubilees of Queen Victoria in 1887 and 1897 respectively. There are also information boards, one of which gives details about the trees and the other tells of George Stephenson and his involvement with the Crich Mineral railway. Look over the wall at the second information board and you will see the blocked-up entrance to the tunnel, which took the line under Sandy Lane. The line was opened in 1841 to bring limestone from the Crich Quarry to the lime kilns at Ambergate. It closed in 1957 and the rail was lifted and taken to the Talyllyn Railway in mid Wales for use there. The line had the unusual gauge (for Britain) of 3'3", better known as one metre.

Along The Tors

Follow the path along the cliff edge and out onto The Tors. This is a gritstone edge, which commands enormous views to the east and west. Looking back you can see the edge of Crich Quarry with Crich Stand perched on the hilltop. Enjoy the stroll along the Tors until you descend steeply to the lane at

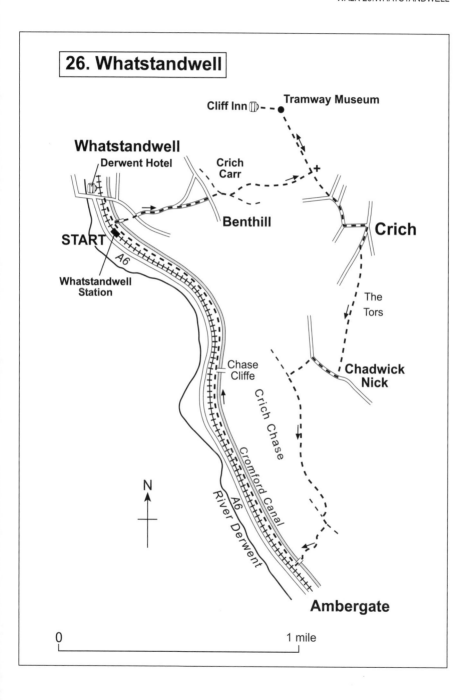

26. Whatstandwell

Cliff Inn -- Tramway Museum

Whatstandwell
Derwent Hotel

Crich
Carr

Benthill

Crich

START

A6

**Whatstandwell
Station**

The
Tors

Chase
Cliffe

**Chadwick
Nick**

Crich Chase

Cromford Canal

N

A6

River Derwent

Ambergate

0   1 mile

Chadwick Nick. The Crich Mineral railway used to cross this road on the level about 100 yards to the left.

Go right at the road and pass through the Nick. Take care as there's no footway (but there are traffic lights – an unusual feature on a road like this, though at the time this walk was recce'd they didn't seem to be working). Once through the Nick there's a good view over the Derwent valley to Shining Cliff Woods and Alderwasley Hall. Go down the road to the right-hand bend and then go left, over a stile and back into fields. Follow the path down by the wall to the brink of the Derwent valley and the edge of Crich Chase. Go left (the path to the right is not a public footpath) and skirt the edge of the valley, accompanied by the dull hum of traffic on the A6 far below.

Through Crich Chase Wood
The path is well-trodden and easy to follow as it enters the oak and birch woodland of Crich Chase. This is a beautiful section of the walk, especially in springtime. The broad path twists and turns its way through the wood. Numerous other paths join and leave, but the main route is always obvious and waymarked in places. You eventually come into a more open area, with a ruined building to your left. Continue straight on until the path bears right to a gateway and begins to descend more steeply, soon re-entering the wood.

Crich Stand

Here the route runs in a pronounced hollow-way, which bears left to join another track at a scissors cross "roads". Don't take the broad track to the left or right, but follow the waymarked path and bear right on the continuation of the hollow-way. Continue the descent. The hollow-way can be very wet and muddy after heavy rain so you may need to deviate from the main route to avoid the worst bits. All being well you should end up at a waymarked stile and gate at the edge of the wood.

The path bears right and goes down the middle of the overgrown field to a gate in the bottom left-hand corner. This leads out onto a rough track. Note the well on the left.

Along the Cromford Canal

Go right, crossing the canal bridge, and then go right again onto the towpath. There used to be a wharf here and there's still a half-sunken boat on the far side of the canal. The boat has two pointed ends to avoid the need for turning. It has deteriorated considerably since this book was first published in 1991, and it had sunk many years before that. Whereas it could have been a restoration project at one time, it is doubtful whether it would be worthwhile now.

The remainder of the walk needs little description as it consists of walking along the towpath back to Whatstandwell station.

This is a delightful stretch of canal, now sadly disused, but a haven for wildlife. The Cromford Canal was opened in 1794, the main traffic being coal and limestone. It enjoyed a modest level of prosperity until the railways came, then like many canals, it was leased to a railway company, in this instance the Midland Railway, in 1852. It was finally purchased outright in 1870. By 1899, traffic at the Cromford end was down to less than 400 tons of coal upwards and less than 1000 tons of stone downwards. The collapse of the Butterley tunnel in 1900 (caused by mining subsidence) ended the through traffic and the local trade soon dwindled to nothing. The canal was officially "abandoned" by the LM&S Railway in 1944, but was taken into national ownership in 1948 and then passed to Derbyshire County Council. Under county council auspices the canal is now managed as a nature reserve and leisure resource. Consider yourself unlucky if you don't spot numerous different kinds of bird on your stroll back to Whatstandwell.

The canal closely parallels the railway line and you soon come to Whatstandwell station. Go left here and cross the footbridge over the line to arrive back on the platform. If you are keen to see if the Derwent Hotel is open before you catch your train or bus, or go for your car, carry on along the towpath for a short way. Once past the wharf go left onto the road and down to the pub. The same applies if you parked your car at the canal bridge on the Crich road.

Walk 27. Winster

The Route	Winster Bank Top, Islington Lane, Elton Cross, Dudwood Lane, (Robin Hood's Stride), Rocking Stone Farm, Uppertown, Ivy House, Winster, Winster Bank Top
Distance	3.9 miles (6¼ km). 770 feet of ascent, (235 metres). Add 1.1 miles (1.8 km) and 315 feet (96 metres) ascent if visiting Robin Hood's Stride. Allow 2 to 2½ hours exclusive of stops. Add at least another hour if visiting Robin Hood's Stride
Grade	Moderate. A visit to Robin Hood's Stride makes it a more serious prospect
Start	car park at the top of West Bank. Map reference: 238602. Public transport users will start from Winster village centre
Map	OS Explorer OL24 The Peak District, White Peak Area
How to get there by bus	There's a Monday to Saturday service from Matlock and Bakewell to Winster (Hulleys 172), but not to Bank Top. Alight in the centre of the village. There's NO Sunday or Bank Holiday Monday service
How to get there by car	From the north, use the A6 to Piccory Corner then follow the B5056 to Winster Bank Top. From the south, A6 to Cromford, then A5012 to Grangemill and then B5056 to Bank Top. From Matlock, A6 to Darley Dale then B5057 to Winster. There's a small car park at the top of West Bank, close to Bank Top. Please do not park in the village, as it gets very congested

The Pub

The Miners Standard

The featured pub is the Miners Standard (tel: 01629 650279) at Winster Bank Top. For those who relate the word 'standard' to flags it is surprising to see the inn sign depicting a dish. The ore dish was the standard measure given to the lead miners by the monarch, hence the name. The dish would have been checked by the senior official of the lead miners' court, the Barmote, and every lead miner had to prove that his mine was capable of supplying a dish of good

The Miner's Standard

ore before being allowed to continue working. The standard dish is still kept at the Barmote Court in Wirksworth. The multi-roomed pub is replete with mining memorabilia.

The Miners Standard is usually open from 12 noon until 4pm and from 7pm on Mondays to Saturdays and 12 noon all day on Sundays. Food is available in the bar or in the dining room from 12 noon till 2:30pm every day and from 7:00pm until 8:30pm Monday to Thursday; on Friday and Saturday night, food is served till 9:00pm. No food on Sunday evenings.

Black Sheep and Marston's Pedigree are the regular draught beers but there's always a selection of guest real ales, many from small Micro-Breweries. The beer selection will always include a 'premium ale' and a weaker 'session ale' for those who prefer a lighter, more quaffable drink. Some recent Guest Beers include offerings from Adnam's, Fullers and Wadworth's. Families and well-behaved dogs are welcome.

The Walk

Islington Lane, Dudwood Lane and a pub with no beer

Winster Bank Top is a separate hamlet clustered around the crossroads formed by the B5056 and the minor roads known as West Bank and Elton

Common Road. There are a couple of farms, a restored 'ore' house and the Miners' Standard pub. The car park has an information panel, which is worth reading. From the car park, go up to the crossroads at the top of the hill and bear right, up the Elton Common road. Away to your left is the Mere and closer to hand is the restored ore house, a reminder of Winster's lead mining past. At the next cross roads turn right again, onto a narrow rough lane, signed as the Limestone Way. This is Islington Lane, at one time an important route and part of the Derbyshire Portway. The lane soon forks and here you keep right. Soon you enter a good example of a hollow-way, constrained between drystone walls. There are fine views across to Wardlow Hay Cop, Stanton Moor and your first glimpse of Robin Hood's Stride.

The lane descends steadily to a cross "roads". Keep straight on here, still on the Limestone Way, climbing slightly before descending again to another crossroads. This is Elton Cross. A pub once stood on the opposite corner, but it ceased to exist when the "new" road was built in the 18th century. Excavations of the site in the late 1980s revealed that the cellars were empty.

A quick left and right here takes you onto a continuation of the narrow lane and a steepening descent. This is Dudwood Lane, again part of the old Portway. The overgrown hillocks of Portway Mine lie to your right. Follow the lane past Dudwood Farm and down to the bottom of the hill. There have been glimpses of Robin Hood's Stride throughout the walk so far and now the time has come to decide whether to visit this fascinating spot. If you choose not to visit the Stride, turn right at the bottom of Dudwood Lane to reach the main road.

Robin Hood's Stride

At the bottom of Dudwood Lane, the path and track straight ahead leads up to the Stride. Including this in the walk adds nearly 1½ miles (2km) to the distance and at least an hour to the time.

The Stride has been an important site since earliest times. To the north lie the Iron Age hill fort of Castle Ring and the Harthill Moor Stone Circle. Below the Stride was a Romano-British settlement, whilst on the flat land between the Stride and Cratcliffe Tor was a small village surrounded by a ditch and palisade. The ditch can still be traced. On the southern slopes of the Tor is the Hermit's cave, sheltered by two ancient yew trees. The cave has a sleeping bench and a carved crucifix; whilst on the rock outside there are channels in the stone to guide water away from the cave, into containers. The hermit apparently gave spiritual succour to the weary travellers on the Portway, the ancient route that passes between the Stride and the Tor. From a distance the Stride gives the impression of being a huge building and its other name is Mock Beggars Hall.

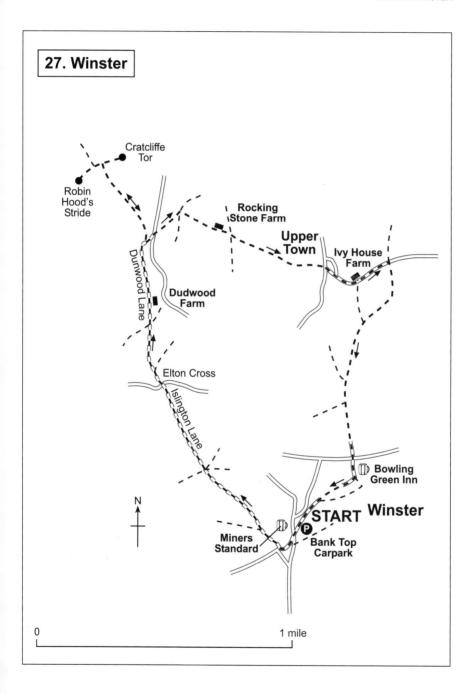

27. Winster

Cratcliffe Tor

Robin Hood's Stride

Rocking Stone Farm

Upper Town

Ivy House Farm

Dunwood Lane

Dudwood Farm

Elton Cross

Islington Lane

Bowling Green Inn

N

START Winster

Miners Standard

Bank Top Carpark

0   1 mile

Robin Hood's Stride

The Stride and its companion pile of rocks, Cratcliffe Tor have been the playgrounds of climbers for many years. The twin towers of the Stride are called The Weasel and the Inaccessible Pinnacle. Apart from the two rock towers the summit rocks are an easy scramble and offer magnificent views. However, scrambling on rocks is not without its dangers and there are well-hidden crevices and polished sections to trap the unwary. However tempting to children (of all ages), please be vigilant and don't attempt either of the towers unless you are a competent climber. And note that the MWS who carved his initials so deeply into The Weasel is not one of the authors of this book!

Robin Hood must have been a giant of a man because the Stride he is supposed to have taken is between the two rock towers! In a cave below the Inaccessible Pinnacle is the so-called "Giant's footprint", but even a chap capable of leaving a footprint of this size would have had some difficulty in striding between the two towers – unless he wore seven league boots.

Leave the Stride and the Tor with reluctance and retrace your steps to the bottom of Dudwood Lane where you turn left to reach the main road.

Along the Birchover by-pass

At the main road, turn left. Cross the road and continue along the verge for about 120 yards (110 metres), to a gate and path signed to Birchover. There's a small section of boardwalk to negotiate a "damp" patch, then another gate before the path goes steeply up the hillside to a gate and stile. Here there's a junction of paths. Go right and then immediately left up a signed footpath, passing to the right of the clump of pines. The Rocking Stones are to your left but are inaccessible (and apparently they no longer rock). You soon come to a ruined building, which has made good use of natural outcrops of rock for its back wall. The holes for roof beams can be seen clearly and the grooves for the roof and water channels are very reminiscent of the ones on the Hermit's Cave on Cratcliffe Tor.

The path keeps to the southern edge of the ridge and the ground to the right falls away steeply. As you pass Rocking Stones Farm, there's a view across to Birchover village. At a crossing of paths keep straight on, following the path along the edge and through a series of fields until you emerge onto the Birchover-Winster lane at Uppertown. (Just to the left here is a set of stocks – of potential use if you have recalcitrant members of your party.)

Cross the road and go up the flight of steps opposite, passing through the yard of Cowley Knoll Farm to reach Clough Lane. Turn right here and follow the lane round the bend where there's a grand view across the valley to Winster. Continue along the lane, ignoring the footpath on the right and soon reaching Ivy House. Just beyond Ivy House, where the lane begins to descend slightly, a footpath crosses the route. Go right here, over a step stile and into fields. One of the stones in the step stile has the word "Beattie" neatly carved into it.

"Causey" stones and bogs

Keeping the wall and hedge to your left go through the field, passing to the left of the curious mound, until you come to the spoil heaps of an erstwhile lead mine. There's a grand view down the valley from here, with Riber Castle very prominent. The path skirts to the left of the spoil heaps, soon reaching a stile at the head of a steep descent. You now enter Stoop Wood. The path bears right, passing a large conical depression on the left. This is probably a run-in shaft, so don't investigate more thoroughly. You leave the wood by a gate in a fence and go steeply down the field to another gate in a fence. Bear right across the next field to a stile by a gate.

Continue downhill, with Winster now in view on the opposite hillside. However, there are a few more trials yet to come. The path descends a steep muddy bank to a streamlet, where there are the remnants of a paved way. The paving continues briefly beyond the stream and the path is obvious enough as it swings first left then right, around the hillside. You then descend again into a boggy area, across which there's (mercifully) a line of "causey" stones.

There has been considerable restoration of this path since the walk was first recce'd, but there's still need to take care, especially in icy weather, when the stones can be slippery. Beyond the bog the paved path continues up to a stile and gate. Follow the well-blazed path across the field to yet another gate, noting that the causey stones have not been restored on this section, which is a pity, as they still seem to exist. Another stretch of field path and another gate land you onto a track close to the children's play area. The track becomes a narrow lane, hemmed in by houses and thus you reach Winster Main Street, by the village shop and post office.

The delights of Winster

At one time, at the height of the lead-mining boom, Winster reputedly had more pubs than Chesterfield. Now however, the lead industry has departed and commuters have discovered the village, as the solidly parked-up main street testifies. The Market Hall is owned by the National Trust and is well worth a visit.

Go left towards the Market Hall, then right, up East Bank. Just before you turn into East Bank, look over the doorway of the last house on the right at the unusual inscription. The Old Bowling Green pub is on your left as you go up East Bank and a decision has to be taken whether to venture in or resist the temptation. Where East Bank forks, go right (signed as a "No through road") and continue to climb. As you climb keep a sharp look out on your right for another pub sign, this time for The Crown with Bertie Hawley named as the licensed victualler. Alas, despite the sign, there's no such pub nowadays. When you reach what seems to be the end of the road, a broad flight of steps leads up to the left and then bears right, passing the Methodist chapel, built in 1823. The path continues onwards and upwards, first as steps, then a path and soon emerging onto a narrow road. Go right here. Winster Bank Top and the Miners' Standard lie about 300 yards (275 metres) along the lane.

Walk 28. Wirksworth

The Route	Wirksworth, Boggart's Inn Farm, Hardhurst, Broadgates, Alport Heights, Hillside Farm, Doveswood Farm, Gorseybank, Wirksworth
Distance	5 miles (8 km). 862 feet of ascent, (263 metres). Allow 2½ to 3 hours exclusive of stops
Grade	Moderate with a number of climbs
Start	Wirksworth Market Place. Map reference: 295540
Map	OS Explorer OL24 The Peak District, White Peak Area
How to get there by bus	There are daily buses to Wirksworth from Ashbourne, Bakewell, Derby, Sheffield and Matlock
How to get there by car	From Matlock follow A6 to Cromford then A5012 and B5023 to Wirksworth. From Derby follow A6 to Duffield then B5023 to Wirksworth. Pay and display parking in the Market Place. Free on-street parking on B5023 north and south of the Market Place, if you can find any
How to get there by train	There are seasonal passenger train services from Duffield to Wirksworth under the auspices of Wyvern Rail, so you can get from all parts of the country to Wirksworth with a change of trains at Duffield

The Pubs

The Black's Head

The Black's Head (tel: 01629 823257) stands in the market place of Wirksworth, a narrow pub with steps up from the pavement to its one main bar. The pub is said to date from the 1700s and has a beamed roof in the bar. The open fire in winter is very welcoming. The room has several little corners away from the central bar, which serves Greene King beers, plus seasonal and guest ales. It is a very traditional house, which serves mainly regulars, but walkers are always made welcome.

The Black's Head is open from 12 noon until 2pm and 5.30pm onwards on Mondays to Fridays. It is open all day Saturdays and on Sunday 12 noon until 3pm and from 7pm onwards. Food is served Mondays to Saturday lunchtimes from 12 noon until 1.45pm. Children are only allowed in the pub at lunchtimes if they are dining. Walkers need to remove muddy boots and clean dogs are also welcome.

Hope and Anchor
The Hope and Anchor (01629 823340) is on the opposite side of the Market Place to the Black's Head. The resident beer is the excellent Tribute from St Austell. There are normally two other guest beers. The pub prides itself on featuring local guest beers, especially the products of the Wirksworth Brewery (try the Anchor Bitter, specially brewed for the pub). Other offerings in the recent past have been Bateman's Summer Swallow, Derby Brewing Co products and some Storm brewery ales from Macclesfield. The pub also serves food and has a beer garden.

Royal Oak
If you are staying in the Wirksworth area then it is also worth trying the Royal Oak (tel: 01629 823000) which sells a range of real ales. It is a friendly, old-fashioned pub, which caters mainly for locals, but walkers are welcome. The pub cannot accommodate children and does not serve food. It is open from 8pm onwards on Mondays to Saturdays and Sunday trading hours are from 12 noon until 3.30pm and from 7.30pm onwards.

The Walk

The delights of Wirksworth
Wirksworth is an ancient market town, with origins back in Saxon times or even earlier. The town itself is situated on the limestone, but to the east rise the shale and gritstone hills of Black Rocks, Bole Hill and Alport Heights. The name "Bole Hill" provides a clue to the town's earlier economic base, which was the production of lead. The lead ore (galena) was extracted from the numerous lead veins in the limestone and was then smelted in primitive furnaces, known as boles, on the nearby gritstone hills.

Wirksworth is still heavily influenced by the minerals industry, though the lead mines have gone and the local quarries have closed. The town still retains the headquarters of the lead mining court, The Barmote. This adjudicates on mineral disputes, using law that has its origins in Roman mineral law.

Wirksworth is full of fine buildings, has an excellent heritage centre and is home to two preserved railways; the Ecclesbourne Valley Railway and the Steeple Grange Light Railway as well as the National Stone Centre, so it is worth visiting.

Aspire for the church

The walk starts from the market place by going over the pedestrian crossing and down the main street. Almost immediately you turn left into a narrow alleyway, which leads into the churchyard. This is rather like a cathedral close

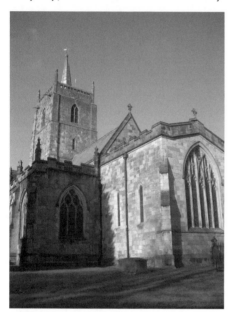

as buildings surround the church. The almshouses and the old grammar school are particularly fine examples. If only the church spire was more dramatic. A church of such quality and setting deserves better than the paltry appendage that currently tops the tower. The church is dedicated to St. Mary and hosts some very fine Saxon carvings depicting the Last Supper, the life of Christ and also lead mining. Well worth a visit either at the start or end of the walk.

Pass to the right of the church and leave the close by the path to the right of the almshouses. Squeeze between the bollards and follow the path down the side of the playing fields to the railway line and turn right.

Wirksworth church

The Wirksworth branch

The Wirksworth branch line has had a chequered history. It was originally envisaged as part of a main line from Derby to Manchester, but never reached beyond Wirksworth and spent most of its time as a minor branch line. The regular passenger service ceased in 1947, so for once, you can't blame Dr Beeching. Mineral traffic from the quarries was always the mainstay of the line and this continued for many years until it was finally diverted to road. The line was then left "mothballed" in the hope of returning mineral traffic, but this never materialised. When this book was first published in 1991, the line was still officially open, but "someone" had removed half a mile of track

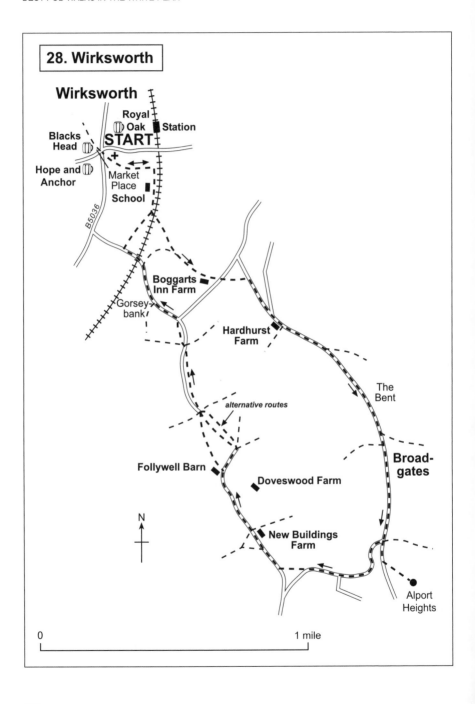

at a strategic point. Now however, the line is in the hands of the Ecclesbourne Valley Railway and has been reopened, so you can now get to Wirksworth by train again.

Follow the path alongside the railway to the point where a path diverges to the left to a stone bridge across the infant Ecclesbourne. The path is signed to Griggs Gardens and Gorseybank. Once over the bridge, go right, alongside the stream to a new stile, then left, up steps to cross the railway line. The path crosses the railway on the level, so take care.

Onwards and upwards

On the far side of the railway, go over another stile and bear right up the field, making for a gap in the hedge. The path is indistinct here, but beyond the gap you head up towards a clump of Scot's Pines. There's a stile and gateway to the right of the pines. Beyond this stile, turn left, joining a track coming up from Gorseybank, the houses of which can be seen to the right.

The track now goes steadily uphill. Where the track turns right towards Boggart's Inn Farm (delightful name), you go straight on, between fences, heading for an obvious gate and stile.

From here there's a fine view back over Wirksworth to Middleton Top, readily distinguished by the chimney of the winding engine. Continue up hill by the fence. Almost at the top of the field there's a little gate on the left. This is the line of the path. (The larger gate immediately in front of you (and very inviting) is surmounted with barbed wire, which rather indicates that you are not welcome to use it). Go through the little gate and turn right. You have a choice of two stiles close by one another to enable you to reach the sanctuary of the lane.

Go left up the lane for a very short way, then right, through a tricky stile and back into fields. There's no obvious path in these fields, but simply head up the hill, keeping well to the left of the farm. Cross the farm access and go through another squeeze stile into another field. The exit can be seen ahead; a squeezer stile leading out onto a lane.

Along the Portway to Alport Heights

Once on the lane, go right. An easy stroll takes you up to the road junction near Hardhurst Farm. There are fine views to the right over the Ecclesbourne valley and back to Wirksworth, with the white of the limestone standing out starkly. This lane was probably part of the old Portway, from which Alport takes its name. The name has nothing to do with the sea. It is derived from "portage" and means "carrying". The masts on top of Alport Heights are now in view ahead.

Continue along the lane, which sees very little traffic, keeping straight on at each junction and rising steadily. After about a mile (1.5 km), you will reach a crossroads at Alport Heights. This is a former beacon site and now used by Derbyshire police as the site of their radio masts. Carry on for a short way, and then go left, up the track towards the masts, then right, into the National Trust car park. The view from here is extensive. Southwards, the power stations of the Trent valley can be seen clearly, and beyond them the line of hills that mark Charnwood Forest. Northwards the vista takes in Harboro' Rocks and much of the White Peak, with glimpses of the higher gritstone moors beyond.

Walk through the car park; skirting the edge of the old gritstone quarry, then descend to the right, still on the quarry edge, to pass the massive standing stone. There are various dates carved into the stone, one obvious example right at the top being G. Waterfield, with a date of 1883. Go back to the road via a narrow path through the gorse, thus passing a stone guidepost. This was erected in 1710 and points the way to Derby and Ashbourne. Note the

Standing stone, Alport Heights

spelling of Derby and Ashbourne. In 1710 this was the main road to Derby from Wirksworth and the big standing stone probably served as a marker as it can be seen prominently from the Portway many miles to the south. Once at the lane bear right, soon reaching the crossroads again. Now, you turn left.

Lost lanes and place names

This lane was presumably formerly the road to Ashbourne mentioned on the guide stone. The lane drops steeply towards the Ecclesbourne valley. The name "Ecclesbourne" is thought to derive from the Latin "ecclesia", which is the root word for the Welsh "eglwys" and the French "église", both meaning "church". Its occurrence in England as the place name "Eccles" normally denotes a Christian church or community persisting through the late Roman period and Dark Ages into early Saxon times.

At the next road junction, keep right and continue to descend Mallinscommon Lane until it swings left. At this point a sign-posted path continues straight ahead, dropping steeply down the field to emerge on another lane alongside Severn Trent's Ashleyhay booster station by a couple of awkward stiles. Go right here, along the narrow lane, passing Hillside Farm on the left and New Buildings Farm on the right. Soon the lane begins to descend quite steeply into the valley of Doveswood Brook with some new woodland planting to the right.

Choice of three

At the bottom of the hill the lane swings right and crosses the brook on a little bridge. Follywell Barn is on the left, but is shown on the OS map as Holehouse Farm. You now have a choice of three routes – unprecedented.

Just over the bridge there's a footpath sign on the left pointing you up a flight of steps that seem to go through the garden of Follywell Barn. This path soon gains open fields and you go straight up the hill, bearing slightly right as you reach the top, and so reaching Prathall Lane at a sharp bend.

Alternatively, you can carry on along the lane, soon passing Doveswood Farm entrance on your right. Here the lane degenerates into a rough track and every time the authors have used it, it has been decidedly muddy. It runs between the fields as a deep cut hollow-way, a sure sign of antiquity and previous heavy use. Even now farm vehicles and four-wheel drive enthusiasts use it, so unless you are feeling particularly masochistic, then the "third way" might be for you.

The third option begins at the entrance to Doveswood Farm. To the left of the entrance and to the right of the lane is a stile. This leads into fields and the footpath runs alongside the hollow-way mentioned previously. The path is not obvious on the ground, but the stiles are all in place and the hollow-way is an unerring guide.

Path and hollow-way continue side by side to a pronounced zigzag. When this walk was first checked, back in 1991, the "zag" contained two ruts of monumental proportions, both filled with water. This has not changed! The path from Follywell Barn emerges onto the lane at this point, but you can gain the safety of a relatively dry path by crossing the lane and going through a stile almost opposite, where you meet up with the path coming up from Doveswood Farm.

Continue on this path, alongside the lane until you come to a stile on the left, where you descend to the hollow-way. Immediately on the other side of the lane is another stile and the path recommences. Bear right, across the field, with the hollow-way now to your right.

Into Gorseybank and back to Wirksworth

This path interlude only lasts for a single field before you rejoin the lane for a final muddy descent into Gorseybank. Bear left at the T-junction. Soon the mud gives way to tarmac and you pass through the older part of Gorseybank, which boasts some very fine former mill buildings, Providence Mill being a classic example.

Follow the road down, passing the Catholic church on the left and then bearing right through the more modern housing. Continue on the road, which now turns left and descends to the railway level crossing.

Just beyond the level crossing, turn right into Brooklands Avenue, signposted to Coldwell Street and the town centre. At the end of the road a tarred path continues beside the railway line and you soon rejoin your outward route. Retrace your steps back to Wirksworth Market Place for a well-earned pint.

Walk 29. Youlgreave (Bradford Dale)

The Route	Youlgreave, Bradford, Bleakley Dike, Harthill Moor, Bleakley Plantation, Hopping Farm, Bradford Dale, Holy Well, Youlgreave
Distance	3.9 miles (6.3 km). 787 feet of ascent (242 metres) Allow 2½ hours exclusive of stops
Grade	Moderate
Start	George Hotel, Youlgreave. Map reference: 212644
Map	OS Explorer OL24 The Peak District, White Peak Area
How to get there by bus	There's a good service from Bakewell to Youlgreave on Mondays to Saturdays (Hulley's 171). There's a sparse Sunday service (Hulley's 181). Alight at Youlgreave church
How to get there by car	Use the A6 to Piccory Corner, then the B5056 to Hawley's Bridge, then the unclassified road to Youlgreave. Youlgreave is signed from the A6. There's a pay/display car park at the western end of the village at Coldwell End. Otherwise there's very limited on-street parking in the village so please park considerately

The Pub

The George

The George Hotel in Youlgreave (tel: 01629 636292) is a homely sort of place, which used to be a Home Brewery pub but now sells a range of beers. There are two principal rooms. On the left is a tap room and on the right a lounge with more formal seating in the bay window area. It is steeped in tradition and so change is slow. The only major change in recent years is the pub sign, which depicts four Royal Georges and their period on the throne from George 1 from 1714 through to George IV in 1820. Talking of royalty, Prince Charles called into the pub some years back with Princess Alexandra for a toilet break and had photos taken with the then landlord.

The George has a number of beers on tap from Theakston's. An extensive food menu is available throughout the day to mid evening. The pub is open all day and every day, so is handy to call in after a walk whatever time you arrive back.

The Walk
Youlgreave to Bradford in 5 minutes
From the George Hotel, cross over the main road and go down the lane ahead towards Bradford on the Bradford Road. The place name "Bradford" presumably derives from "Broad ford". The church of All Saints stands to your left. Part way down the hill, the road forks. Bear right here, along the lane where the sign proclaims the route is unsuitable for motor vehicles. At the bottom of the hill the road swings left, alongside the River Bradford. However, you go ahead to traverse the stone footbridge, noting the strip of grass on the far side. There used to be a garage here, which could only be approached by driving the car into the water. Follow the path to the road.

Turn right, along the road. In 100 yards/metres, opposite a row of houses, there's a stile/gate on the left, signposted as the Limestone Way. Go through the stile/gate and bear slightly right.

Clapper bridge, Bradford

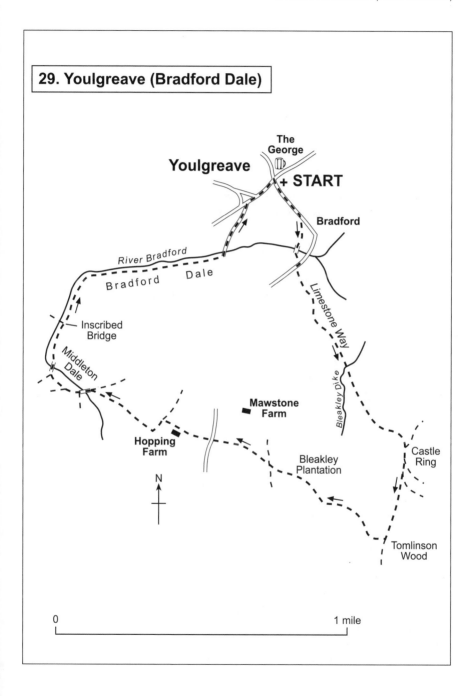

29. Youlgreave (Bradford Dale)

The
George

Youlgreave

+ START

Bradford

River Bradford

Bradford Dale

Limestone Way

Inscribed
Bridge

Middleton Dale

Bleakley Dike

**Mawstone
Farm**

**Hopping
Farm**

**Bleakley
Plantation**

**Castle
Ring**

N

Tomlinson
Wood

0   1 mile

Castle Ring and Mawstone Mine

The flat-topped hill that dominates the scene ahead is Castle Ring, an Iron Age hill fort. Your path leads unerringly towards it. On the hillside to the right you can discern the grassed over spoil heaps of Mawstone Mine. This lead mine closed in 1932 following a gas explosion, which killed eight miners. Such explosions were commonplace in coalmines, but were extremely rare in lead mines, as these were mainly in limestone. However, the mines between Bradford Dale and the Derwent at Darley Dale were worked through shales and gritstones and were prone to "firedamp".

Go through a gate to follow the well-blazed path. Go slightly right and through a gap stile, always heading towards Castle Ring. You join a track, which bends right and left up to a barred gate. Pass through the right-hand gateway and continue alongside the wall to a stile. Now the path bears slightly right towards the electricity pole and then descends to cross the Bleakley Dike. This approach can be decidedly muddy, despite carefully positioned stones. A stile now follows and then the path begins the climb towards Castle Ring. Follow the broad green path up the hill to the old gap stile and at this point bear left on a track, just to the right of a solitary oak tree. The track now swings away to the left, climbing gently and then bends right, into a shallow valley below Castle Ring.

Follow the track below Castle Ring through a gateway, ignoring the footpath sign that points up to the fort. Where the track swings left to Harthill Moor Farm, continue straight on, passing a gate on the right and locating a step stile in the wall ahead. Robin Hood's Stride can be seen to the left. From this angle it is easy to see how a traveller might mistake it for a large house. Hence the Stride's other name, Mock Beggars Hall.

On to Hopping Farm

Once over the stile, head up the field on an indistinct path, making for the right-hand end of Tomlinson's Wood. At the gate and stile by the wood, there's another set of instructions to Hopping Farm. Turn right here and follow the wall to another stile about 150 yards/metres further on. Here bear right, crossing the field to a gate and stile, which is crossed. Follow the wall on your left to a stile in the field corner. In the next field, bear right, passing a small walled enclosure and heading towards Bleakley Plantation. Go through a gap stile and head diagonally through the next field, still towards the wood. Go through a gateway and now the direction of the path changes to run parallel with the boundary of the wood.

The exit stile from this field is to the right of the solitary tree and boasts a signpost. Go slightly right here with a good view to the right over Youlgreave and Bradford. Pass through another gap stile and continue ahead to the crest of the ridge. Here the panorama suddenly opens up as the slope plunges away below you. Cross a stile and follow the path down towards Hopping Farm, whose crop of caravans can be seen below.

Go through a gate to the Bradford-Gratton lane. Cross this and go through a small gate opposite, continuing the descent to Hopping Farm through two more gap stiles. The path is well-signed through the caravan site and you soon reach the farm buildings. Look out for a signpost to Middleton Dale. Do not be put off at this point. The path goes just to the right of the farmhouse, so please be considerate. You then make your way ahead.

Roller Dale?

Once past the farmhouse you re-enter open fields and descend steadily to the upper reaches of Middleton Dale to cross a stile by a gateway and ahead to cross another stile. On reaching the valley bottom, follow the stream down to a clapper bridge, which, after all these years is still signed to Roller Dale and Gratton although the sign attached to a tree is somewhat weathered now. Even keen aficionados of Derbyshire Dales would be hard pressed to locate Roller Dale, especially as there's no path through it! Why then is it signed?

Bradford Dale

Don't cross the bridge, but continue along the dale. The path is now forced away from the stream by a low limestone cliff, but you soon descend to river level again, by a flight of metal steps. Be careful in damp weather, as the steps can be slippery, to say nothing of the polished limestone approaches.

A short distance down the dale, the path crosses a bridge and swings right, following the river. Just beyond the bridge, the path crosses a sizeable stream, which emerges from the rocks on the left. This helps to drain the Long Rake mines above Middleton. Continue down the dale, to a T-junction. Ignore the path going left towards Middleton and turn right, crossing the river again close to some ruined buildings and sheep-wash pens. The path down the dale now becomes a broad track. Another T-junction is reached and here you join the Limestone Way again. Your route continues down the dale, but pause to have a look at the bridge and the inscription in the parapet wall. It reads, *"Still glides the stream and shall forever glide. The form remains, the function never dies".*

The rest of the walk is a delightful stroll down one of Derbyshire's most beautiful dales, alongside sparkling waters and fish pools. Usually, you would consider yourself unfortunate not to spot dabchicks, herons, moorhens, coots, varieties of duck and even, if you are really lucky, a kingfisher. However, in

2011 the river was almost totally dry so that fish stocks had to be transferred. It remains to be seen if this was a one off event or whether this will become the norm.

When you reach a stone slab bridge, just over ½ mile (1 km) from the inscribed bridge, go left and cross the river to reach the foot of Holy Well. This lane gives a quick ascent to the centre of Youlgreave, where a walk up the main street quickly brings you back to The George. Alternatively, you can carry on along the north bank of the river back to Bradford and then retrace your steps up past the church to The George.

Bradford Dale

Walk 30. Youlgreave to Bakewell

The Route	Youlgreave, Conksbury Lane, Raper Lodge, Over Haddon, Noton Barn Farm, Intake Lane, Bakewell
Distance	4¼ miles (6¾ km). 380 feet of ascent, (117 metres). Allow 2 to 2½ hours exclusive of stops
Grade	Moderate walk with a few climbs
Start	Youlgreave church (if arriving by bus). Map reference: 212644
Map	OS Explorer OL24 The Peak District, White Peak Area
How to get there by bus	There's a good service from Bakewell to Youlgreave on Mondays to Saturdays (Hulley's 171). There's a sparse Sunday service (Hulley's 181). Alight at Youlgreave church
How to get there by car	As this is a linear walk you'll have to use the bus at some stage. The suggestion is that you park in Bakewell and catch the bus to Youlgreave. You shouldn't need any help in finding Bakewell (and if you do, your navigational skills will be seriously tested on any of these walks). The main car parks lie on the north side of the river and are clearly signed from the A6 and the A619. If you insist on driving to Youlgreave, use the A6 to Piccory Corner, then the B5056 to Hawley's Bridge, then the unclassified road to Youlgreave. Youlgreave is signed from the A6. There's very limited on-street parking in the village so please park considerately

The Pubs

The Lathkil Hotel
The Lathkil Hotel (tel: 01629 812501) in Over Haddon is not to be missed. This long-standing Good Beer Guide entry must have some of the finest views of the surrounding countryside and into the Lathkill Dale National Nature Reserve. The bar is very appealing, with traditional oak panelling and a fire

Enjoying a jar at Lathkil Hotel

offering a warm glow during winter months. There's also a more formal dining room and families are welcome. Walkers are asked to remove muddy boots. I think you need to read the signs carefully to get the message-you really do need to take your boots off. There's an outside covered seating area where you can do just that but don't be put off for the beer is good, as befits a pub that has featured so long in the Good Beer Guide. There's also a beer garden, which is delightful in the summer months.

The main bar offers a range of beers on hand pull including Hartington Bitter from the Whim Brewery and many other locally sourced brews. The hotel is open from 11am until 3pm and from 6.30pm on weekdays in the winter and all day during the weekends and on other days in summer. Food is served between 12 noon and 2pm (2.30pm at weekends) and from 7pm to 9pm in the evenings. Overnight accommodation is available and updates are available on www.lathkil.co.uk. All in all, this is a lovely place for the walker to stop awhile.

Other pubs en route
The walk starts in Youlgreave at The George Hotel (see Walk 29 for description). On arrival in Bakewell you are spoilt for choice. Within a couple

of minutes walk of the old bridge you've got The Castle (01629 812103), The Queen's Arms (01629 814586), The Peacock (01629 813635), The Red Lion (01629 812054), The Wheatsheaf (01629 812985) and slightly further away on Haddon Road (A6), The Manners (01629 812756). All serve at least one real ale and food.

The Walk

Time is no object

When you alight from the bus take time to observe the church, which stands steadfastly in the middle of the village. It is a timeless scene for the tower clock, built in 1870, shows 12 minutes to 10 whatever the day or the time of day. We hope that time has moved on by the time you're sampling this superb little linear walk. Start the ramble with your back to the entrance to the George Hotel. Go right and right again on the lane towards Conksbury. Turn first right by Easter Cottage and White House on a narrow lane, which is shown as a 'No Through Road'. Pass by Raper Lodge on the right and go over the ornate footbridge, which spans the waters of the Lathkill. Now climb a zig-zag path into woodland, winding your way over root and rock to a bridle gate.

Once through, go right, across the field towards a barn and sheds screened by a line of trees. On reaching another bridle gate, turn to go slightly left. You should now be

Youlgreave church

able to catch sight of Over Haddon in the distance. The Lathkil Hotel is the white building. Cross a stone step stile and go ahead in the next field. Go through a gap stile, cross the road and through another stile. Keep ahead once again and then pass through a gate and follow the line of hawthorns. Below to your left is the River Lathkill, much altered in the past to provide fish pools,

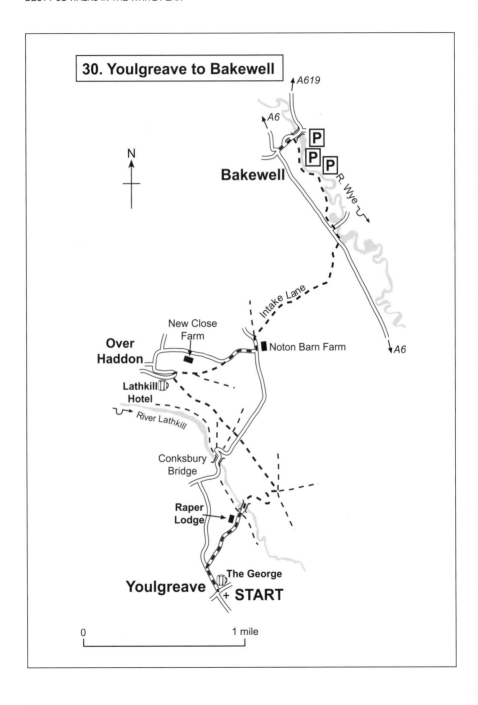

30. Youlgreave to Bakewell

↑A619

↑A6

P P P

R. Wye

Bakewell

N

Intake Lane

New Close
Farm

**Over
Haddon**

■ Noton Barn Farm

**Lathkill
Hotel**

↓A6

River Lathkill

Conksbury
Bridge

**Raper
Lodge**

The George

Youlgreave **START**

0   1 mile

water for mills and scenic walks for the then owners of the Haddon Estate. It is hard to believe now that Lathkill Dale was once also a major mining area. Further up the dale there are remains of mine buildings, wheel pits, shafts, dams and aqueducts. It is a fascinating place. Go through the gate on the right by the fence. Turn left to rise to a stile, which is crossed. Climb again to go through a gap stile, guarded by gates, into the next pasture. As you wander across the next pasture you'll get a great view of Over Haddon. Ahead lies the Lathkil hotel.

Over Haddon

Having imbibed sufficiently of both the view and the ale, leave the pub and turn left to go through the gap stile (and gate) at the end of the lane. Now keep ahead on a path that is less well trodden than those you've been on previously. Cross a stone step stile and head slightly right to another stile. Cross it and head slightly right across the pasture to go through a gate and stone stile onto a lane. Turn right to descend to a T-junction opposite the entrance to Noton Barn Farm. Haddon Park and Manners Wood can be seen clearly from here. Go left and take care to walk facing traffic for a short section of busier road. Once around the corner look for a gate on the right, leading into a pasture. Keep to the right in this field, down to another gate and so onto Intake Lane

Intake Lane

The track descends, for about half a mile (800 metres), between fields and an increasing number of dwellings at the lower end, to reach the main A6 road on the outskirts of Bakewell. Cross the road with care and then go left for about 30 yards/metres before cutting right then left on a path, which skirts the River Wye. This leads to a road known as Agricultural Way (leading to the market, of course). Cross this, then straight ahead on a narrow path, firstly between allotments and then garden hedges and fences. Cross an estate road and continue straight on, into the park and playing field. Follow the tarmac path across the park, before turning right by the public toilets, thus reaching the riverside path. Here turn left and fight your way alongside the river through hordes of visitors feeding the ducks, fish and themselves. There are various routes into the town centre from this thoroughfare, but the suggestion is that you make your way alongside the river to the old road bridge and there turn left. A short stroll takes you into the town centre for the various bus stops, pubs, cafes, shops and all the usual paraphernalia expected of a tourist hotspot.

If you've come to Bakewell by car, the chances are you've parked in one of the car parks on the north bank of the river. Either of the two pedestrian bridges will take you to the Agricultural Centre car park. The second pedestrian bridge will take you to Smith's Island car park and turning right at the road bridge will take you to the Woodyard car park.

Also from Sigma Leisure:

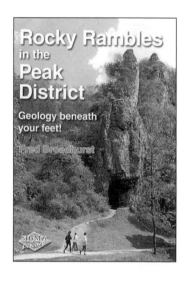

Rocky Rambles in The Peak District
Fred Broadhurst

"The Peak District has a dramatic story to tell and Fred Broadhurst is just the guide we need." – Aubrey Manning, presenter of the BBC TV series 'Earth Story'.

You don't have to be an expert or even an amateur geologist to enjoy these 'rocky rambles'! Where better than in and around the Peak District would you find geology right there beneath your feet - all you need to know is where to look.

The comprehensive glossary of terms, which covers the identification of Peak District Rocks, forms an invaluable supplement and provides 'at a glance' information for the reader.

£8.99

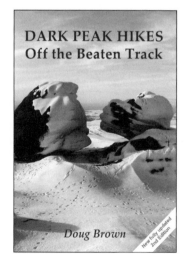

Dark Peak Hikes
Off the Beaten Track
Doug Brown

Here are 30 walks in the Dark Peak - the legendary northern part of the Peak District that covers some of the best hill country of Derbyshire, Yorkshire and Greater Manchester. Renowned for its unique peat ecology and striking gritstone scenery, the Dark Peak is a paradise for adventurous walkers intent on exploring the remoter parts of the moors.

Includes lots of helpful information for each walk – starting point, distance and estimated time, a general description including level of difficulty, and a very detailed route description.

£8.99

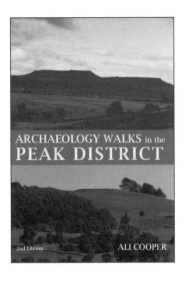

Archaeology Walks in the Peak District
Ali Cooper

Put on your walking boots, enjoy the superb scenery of the Peak District and enjoy a roller-coaster ride through history with Ali Cooper. Routes ranging from 3 to 12 miles explore Peak District sites where there are visible features in the landscape. Brief descriptions of the major finds on the walks are included, plus a bibliography for those who want to delve deeper.

"... a new authoritative book ... for a spot of time travel while out walking" – Derby Evening Telegraph

£8.99

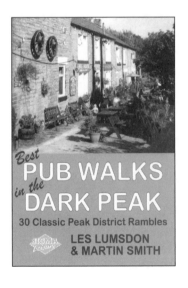

Best Pub Walks in the Dark Peak
30 Classic Peak District Rambles
Les Lumsden & Martin Smith

A large area of Derbyshire is included in the Dark Peak, together with sections of East Cheshire, South Yorkshire and North Staffordshire, and the 30 rambles in this book are based on the very best parts of this wild and characterful region. The walks range from 3 to 11 miles and all start at or call at one of the many Peakland pubs in and around the picturesque villages of the Dark Peak.

Each walk includes information about the locality, yarns and legends of the area as well as general geographical description.

£7.95

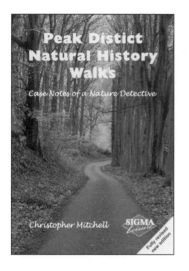

Peak District Walking Natural History Walks
Christopher Mitchell

An updated 2nd Edition with 18 varied walks for all lovers of the great outdoors — and armchair ramblers too! Learn how to be a nature detective, a 'case notes' approach shows you what clues to look for and how to solve them. Detailed maps include animal tracks and signs, landscape features and everything you need for the perfect natural history walk. There are mysteries and puzzles to solve to add more fun for family walks — solutions supplied! Includes follow on material with an extensive Bibliography and 'Taking it Further' sections.

£8.99

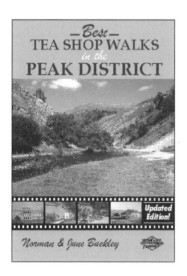

Best Tea Shop Walks in the Peak District
Norman and June Buckley

A wonderful collection of easy-going walks that are ideal for families and all those who appreciate fine scenery with a touch of decadence in the shape of an afternoon tea or morning coffee —or both! The 26 walks are spread widely across the Peak District, including Lyme Park, Castleton, Miller's Dale, and The Roaches and — of course — such famous dales as Lathkill and Dovedale. Each walk has a handy summary so that you can choose the walks that are ideally suited to the interests and abilities of your party. The tea shops are just as diverse, ranging from the splendour of Chatsworth House to more basic locations. Each one welcomes ramblers and there is always a good choice of tempting goodies.

£8.99

Derbyshire Walks with Children
William D Parke

There are 24 circular walks, ranging from 1 to 6 miles in length, and each one has been researched and written with children in mind. The directions and background information have been checked and revised as necessary for this updated reprint.

Detailed instructions for parents and an interactive commentary for children mean there's never a dull moment. There are even 'escape routes' to allow families to tailor each walk to suit their own needs, time and energy.

"The needs, entertainment and safety of children have been of paramount importance."
– Peak Advertiser
£8.99

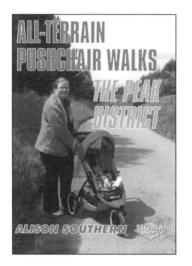

All-Terrain Pushchair Walks: The Peak District
Alison Southern

The Peak District, in the heart of the country, has some of England's most picturesque landscapes, from the White Peak in the south with its rocky outcrops and steep hills, to the Dark Peak in the north with peat moss moorland and stunning vistas. This book is for families with all-terrain pushchairs and buggies, and for everyone wishing to avoid as many stiles and obstacles as possible. Includes family-friendly attractions, trees to identify, birds and plants to spot, and lots more to discover. Have fun while you walk enjoying the amazing views, have some healthy exercise and spend time with the family away from the modern world.
£8.99

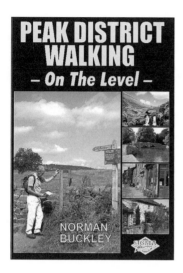

Peak District Walking On The Level
Norman Buckley

Some folk prefer easy walks, and sometimes there's just not time for an all-day romp. In either case, this is definitely a book to keep on your bookshelf. Norman Buckley has had considerable success with "On The Level" books for the Lake District and the Yorkshire Dales.

The walks are ideal for family outings and the precise instructions ensure that there's little chance of losing your way. Well-produced maps encourage everybody to try out the walks - all of which are well scattered across the Peak District.

£8.99

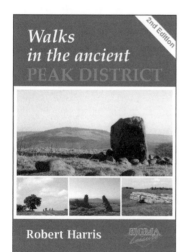

Walks in the Ancient Peak District
Robert Harris

A collection of walks visiting the prehistoric monuments and sites of the Peak District. A refreshing insight into the thinking behind the monuments, the rituals and strange behaviour of our ancestors. All the routes are circular, most starting and finishing in a town or village that is easy to locate and convenient to reach by car.

£8.99

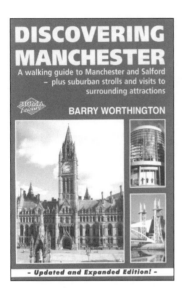

Discovering Manchester
2nd Edition
Barry Worthington

This stylish walking guide doubles as a detailed account of the city's architecture, its history and tourism attractions. There are walks throughout Manchester including such major entertainment and cultural centres as the Bridgewater Hall, Urbis, the Museum of Science and Industry, the Lowry and many more. Explore the entire city – from the Corn Exchange to G-Mex, from the Cathedral to Affleck's Palace.

£10.99

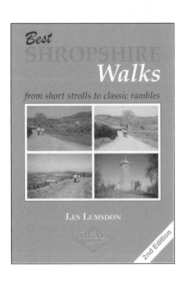

Best Shropshire Walks 2nd Edition
From short strolls to classic rambles
Les Lumsdon

A new revised edition of this much loved guide contains 36 walks, including 12 completely new routes, located in all parts of the county. Several walks feature fine hill walking on the Welsh borders and others start from delightful villages and hamlets in the north and east of the county.

£8.99

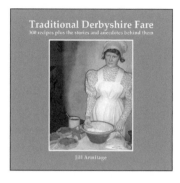

Traditional Derbyshire Fare
300 recipes plus the stories and anecdotes behind them
Jill Armitage

Some Derbyshire dishes are well known, like the Bakewell Pudding; many more, including some of the most delectable, are little known outside the places whose name they bear. The recipes are individual, easy, economical, with readily available ingredients, and have a strong regional accent. This is Derbyshire food at its best.

£12.95

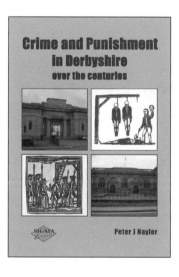

Crime and Punishment in Derbyshire
over the centuries
Peter J Naylor

Crime fascinates us all, particularly murders, and the bloodier they are the better they are received. It would appear that the Peak District was a lawless place until more recent times. This book is a thorough mix of most of the types of crimes committed in Derbyshire over the centuries. Each chapter is dedicated to a different type of crime and the punishments handed out. Whilst this book gives much of its space over to murder, other crimes are also included.

£8.99

All of our books are all available through booksellers. For a free catalogue, please contact:

**SIGMA LEISURE, STOBART HOUSE, PONTYCLERC, PENYBANC ROAD
AMMANFORD, CARMARTHENSHIRE SA18 3HP**
Tel: 01269 593100   Fax: 01269 596116

info@sigmapress.co.uk   www.sigmapress.co.uk